DERBY TRAINMAN

2nd Edition
&
Lost Lines

Tim Helme

Published by

Top Link Press
toplink@btinternet.com

CONTENTS

AUTHOR'S NOTE

I had originally planned to write an article solely on the Denby Branch, but as this work progressed and the information kept coming, I felt it equally important to profile the other major jobs that Derby Trainmen undertook as well. The 'Trainman Concept' was in operation for six years (1988-94), and I did the last four of them. I may not have been present at its conception, but I certainly was at its conclusion. The rail industry has changed enormously since 1994, but to me, it seems to have lost a lot of its heart and soul in the process. In writing this book, I wanted to look back and provide an account of how things used to be done and what it was like to be part of an organisation (or even family) that stretched the length and breadth of the country.

I would like to thank Helen Chadfield, Richard King, Bryn Davies and Philip Helme for their assistance with this edition.

Additional Derby Trainman material (not included in this book) appeared in *Rail Express* over 20-part series from March 2015-October 2016:

'Playing by the rules...'
'Going hands on.'
'Things get messy...'
'Know your onions!'
'Language Timothy!'
'Tough brake!'
'Fright night!'
'What a banker!'
'So the brakes work then?'
'Odds and sods.'
'Signs of trouble.'
'It's your turn son.'
'Put your back into it!'
'From gogglebox to signalbox.'
'Nightshifts on shed.'
'A white-knuckle ride.'
'WAR: what is it good for?'
'Milking it!'
'Like a limestone cowboy.'
'A fistful of dust.'

Also:
'A year at Scropton.' August 2017.
'Calling at Derby.' January 2019.
'On a roll to Royce's.' August 2019.

FOREWORD

By Derby Driver, Richard King, who successfully progressed through the Trainman (D) route of employment during this period.

The grade of Trainman was created during the train crew reorganisation of British Rail in 1988 and was an amalgamation of the traditional grades of Guard and Secondman (Fireman). Around this time a shortage of drivers was foreseen at Derby due to several 'old hands' approaching retirement age, so to cover this shortfall, several new recruits were employed straight 'off the street'. For them to gain experience in this very different, almost Victorian, working environment (of which many steam age practices remained), they were employed in the new grade of Trainman. Those who successfully passed the driver selection course at Manchester were designated Trainman (D). On completion of an eight-week course, the new Trainmen were then let loose upon the railway network covering, as will be seen, a wide variety of jobs on routes emanating from the Derby area.

Derby train crew were based in the remaining buildings of the old Number 4 Shed, of which only the mess room, locker room and various administration offices still stood. During its prime, 4 Shed housed two turntables and was the running shed of the Derby Loco Works complex. By 1990, its status had been vastly reduced, but a range of motive power could still be found stabled there, with classes 08, 20, 31, 37, as well as the ubiquitous class 47, together with HSTs, Sprinters and first generation DMUs, parked in the adjoining Etches Park Carriage Sidings.

Being versatile (able to work both passenger and freight trains), and having the Carriage & Wagon Works, Railway Technical Centre, Economic Oil Terminal and Chaddesden Sidings all within proximity to the depot, no two days were the same for a trainman. But with experience quickly gained (sometimes the hard way!), life on the railway eventually became routine. When the need arose, the senior men of the grade were put forward for driver training, thus covering the predicted shortfall. However, in July 1992, came the announcement that the railways of Britain were to be privatised. This comfortable and settled existence railway employees had grown accustomed to – a way of life – was about to change. Uncertainty was the topic of mess rooms up and down the network, as the railway was broken up into business sectors and now run to satisfy the demands of accountants, rather than the needs of the customers, be it passenger or freight.

The Derby area came under the banner of InterCity Midland Cross Country and, as a result, the workload became greatly reduced, leaving only the departmental ballast trains, RTC test work and the occasional passenger job for the trainmen. Endless hours of sitting spare in the mess room ensued, while only at weekends was there a buzz of activity, when on Saturday evenings, procession after procession of departmental ballast trains left the nearby Chaddesden Sidings en-route to various worksites around the Midlands. This situation could never last and during early 1994, redundancy was offered, of which there were many takers. For those left, life carried as normal for a few months, until a further announcement came that Derby was to become an all-passenger depot and that all non-passenger work, together with the role of Trainman, would cease.

Tim Helme's account of life as a Derby Trainman gives a fascinating insight into those last few years of British Railways. The jobs, the characters and the humour are all here as a lasting reminder.

<u>Derby station area, circa 1990</u>

1. Derby PSB
2. New Sidings
3. 4 Shed
4. Loco Stabling & Wind Tunnel

1. MIXED TRAFFIC

The process of becoming a Trainman (D) was not an easy one and becoming a Trainman (D) at my home depot of Derby was especially difficult. For a start, driving vacancies there were extremely rare, particularly for someone 'straight off the street'. However, towards the end of 1989, fate, or whatever, decreed that I was finally in the right place at the right time, and after my initial application, interview and preliminary test, I was summoned for a formal interview with the Area Train Crew Manager. I must assume that I met his exacting standards because, not long after, I was dispatched to the Train Crew Selection Centre at Manchester Piccadilly for some rather intensive testing. After successfully completing all their mechanical, concentration, observation and reaction tests, and a further interview, I was then sent to the railway doctor at Derby for a medical. After this exhaustive selection process, I was finally offered the position of Trainee Trainman (D) at Derby but would first have to complete my initial training at Toton depot.

Along with several other new starters, I spent eight weeks in a classroom at Toton learning the fine art of railway operation, as taught by British Rail. The first week was an induction course where we became acquainted with the BR Rule Book, as well as the Working Manual (white and pink pages) and the General Appendix. These books became our constant career long companions, as we were always required to carry them when on duty. Successful completion of this first week enabled a new starter to undertake the duties of a yard shunter, and a couple of our classmates who had been employed on this path were dispatched to such locations as Maltby Colliery and Drakelow Power Station to begin their prospective careers. After the induction came the more intensive six-week Trainman (G) course, where all the rules and regulations appertaining to the duties and responsibilities of a BR guard (both freight and passenger) were mercilessly drummed into us. Provided you passed the rules exam at the end, you officially became a qualified guard...in theory at least.

The Rule Book Sections

A. General safety and security responsibilities.
B. Safety when working on or near running lines.
C. Signals.
D. Passing signals at danger, wrong direction working.
H. Working of trains.
J. Shunting.
K. Trains or vehicles detained on running lines or loops.
M. Accidents and failures.
N. Single line working.
R/T. Engineers' responsibilities and protection of work.
U. Temporary and emergency speed restrictions.

An important section of the Rule Book, and a favourite of any examiner, was section M, which dealt with train protection. In the event of an accident or train failure, three detonators, twenty yards apart, had to be placed 300 yards from the train. (Full protection consisted of one at ¼ of a mile, one at ½ a mile and three at a mile and a ¼.) The driver would go forward to protect, whilst the guard or secondman would go back. The brightly coloured detonators contained a small explosive charge and were affixed to the top of the rail. If run over by another train, the resulting detonations would alert that driver to the obstruction ahead. Although there were some in every locomotive cab, train crew also carried a personal issue of ten detonators with them when on duty.

Those of us who had successfully completed the testing at Manchester then progressed on to the final week-long Trainman (D) course, where we were taught all the duties of the driver's assistant, or secondman. There was another test at the end, this time conducted by the resident traction inspector, but after eight weeks of meticulously ploughing through the Rule Book, I found this one to be relatively straightforward. I was now qualified to act as a guard (pending the relevant road knowledge) and a secondman. All I needed now was some solid practical experience, and Derby didn't disappoint.

The end of the trainman course was by no means the end of the learning process. A Ministry of Transport requirement was for all drivers and guards to have detailed knowledge of the routes they worked over. This knowledge obviously included such things as stations, junctions, signals, gradients, speed limits, shunting movements, and so on. Individual routes would be learnt for a set period, at the end of which, the senior train crew supervisor (TCS) expected you to sign your road card confirming that you were competent to work a train over said routes. A trainman carrying out the duties of a secondman was exempt from this rule. He could undertake any secondman work as required, since he (supposedly) always accompanied a driver with the necessary knowledge. On the occasional and unavoidable times where a driver or guard was required to operate over a route they didn't sign, a conductor would have to be provided. Conducting train crew obviously had the necessary knowledge and assisted the booked crew over the route. This method of conducting also applied to the different types of traction a driver might encounter too.

From a trainman's point of view, learning a road was relatively straightforward, but it wasn't enough just to know the names of stations, junctions and nearby settlements between Derby and a certain point. There could be any number of small sidings along the way, or even a major marshalling yard, all with slightly different rules and methods of working, but it was the trainman's job, if he signed the road, to know how to operate in these places – at any time and in any weather. For example, between Derby and Leicester, roughly a distance of 30 miles, there were at least three ballast sidings a Derby trainman would require knowledge of. However, as a certain proportion of our road learning was done from passenger trains, it wasn't always easy to examine these sidings properly.

8

When questioned, most of the drivers you rode with always responded with the famous last words; "That's so and so sidings...don't worry about them, you'll never go in there." So, after a week of road learning, you would happily sign the route, only to find that almost the very next day, you would be working a job to so and so sidings. You could of course sign the road for passenger work only, but trainmen who made a habit of this quite rightly invited much derision for their colleagues. It was a rather selfish way of always ensuring the secondman position on a weekend ballast job, or avoiding a job completely, particularly if it involved too much work. Another practice, just as unprofessional as work avoidance, was developing a blasé attitude towards road learning. Some people signed roads on a whim, often after travelling over them just once. These were the people who usually slipped up, sometimes endangering others. To be fair, much of the work was common sense and learnt through experience, but I always took road learning seriously, because when you have a freight train waiting to clear the main line at 02:00 and you're stood at a ground frame (a set of manual point levers) not knowing which lever to pull, then it's too late.

A good example of how seriously I took road learning was when a group of us were sent to learn the routes between Derby and Sheffield. Most of us already signed as far as Ambergate Junction, so travelling backwards and forwards on passenger trains served our needs adequately enough. However, we needed to study Avenue ground frame and sidings, situated near Clay Cross, but instead of hitching a ride on a freight train, I decided we would stick with the passenger service, alight at Chesterfield station and walk back. Of course, the distance and journey time between the two points didn't seem too terrible from a carriage window travelling at 70mph, but our little walk turned out to be a six-mile round trip on merciless railway ballast. One of my colleagues had just been issued with the latest 'Corporate Collection' railway uniform, including new shoes, which were unfortunately giving him a bit of grief. I think he moaned every step of the way, but had occasion to thank me later, as that same year we ended up working a lot of weekend engineering trains on the Erewash Valley Line, many of which required to be run round using Avenue ground frame.

When I started at Derby at the beginning of 1990, it was still classed as British Rail London Midland Region, and officially remained so until the 5th of April 1992. As the different business sectors emerged as a prelude to privatisation, management embarked on a period of name changing. As the all-encompassing British Rail name was subtly dispensed with, we were classed in part, as East Midlands (Passenger), before finally being designated as an InterCity (Midland Cross Country) depot. Initially, the different names or sectors didn't alter the volume of work to pass through Derby. Passenger services were still as important as ever, and the wealth and variety of freight work was most welcome, particularly from a trainman's point of view. To my knowledge, from 1990 right up to eventual privatisation, Derby Trainmen were involved in almost every sphere of operation, except freightliner and automotive trains. We worked coal, petroleum, metals, chemicals, construction, research, departmental, passenger, and even the mail. Even Toton couldn't boast this range of work. Within a couple of years, my road knowledge extended to all points of the compass to accommodate this mixed traffic. I signed as far as Leeds and York in the north, Nottingham and Peterborough in the east, London St. Pancras in the south, Birmingham and Gloucester in the southwest, and no Derby road card was complete without Crewe in the northwest.

It may have been 1990, but some rules and railway practices hadn't changed much from steam days. Guards' brakevans were still used on trains, but only on two specific types: trains that were unfitted (i.e., without functioning brakes), and trains carrying dangerous goods. However, a noteworthy addition to this rule was our very own 'Denby' job. Brakevans were necessary on this train, simply because of the trainman-operated crossings on the branch, (see Chap. 10). The three categories of dangerous goods where a brakevan would be required were nuclear flasks, hydrocyanic acid and toxic gas. The reason for having a brakevan on this kind of work was quite simple, if a problem occurred with the train (e.g., a fire or derailment), the driver would go forward to carry out detonator protection, whilst the guard, who was already at the rear, would go back. This way, no one would have to pass any potentially unstable or damaged wagons, which was rather important considering the nature of the materials being conveyed.

Derby crews weren't normally responsible for any nuclear flask or hydrocyanic acid traffic, but there were at least two toxic gas jobs allocated to us. These both belonged in the senior trainmans' link (roster), and it would be nearly two years before I progressed from the junior link to such heady and respected heights. The first job was known as the Bromsgrove Tanks, where Derby crew worked the train to and from the sidings at the foot of Blackwell bank (or Lickey incline), southwest of Birmingham. I never got to work this job (not 'officially' anyway), as another depot gained the work before I achieved a place in the top link. However, when I did eventually move up the ladder, I got to work the remaining job many times. This was known as the York Tanks, and potential hazards aside, it was one of my favourites (see Chap. 9). Much to my exasperation though, the two trainman links were merged not long afterwards.

The reason for having a brakevan on unfitted, or partially fitted trains, was that if a coupling broke and the train became divided, the driver would be able to apply the loco brakes and stop his portion, whilst the guard could do likewise in the brakevan. Unfitted trains were restricted to 25mph and partially fitted to 35mph. In the brief period between my starting on the railway and British Rail Engineering Limited being completely lost forever, the Carriage Works at Litchurch Lane retained a contract with London Underground to refurbish their coaching stock. The job consisted of one complete London Underground train, with a barrier wagon at each end. It was unfitted and therefore required a brakevan. The job originated from the London Regional Transport (LRT) depot at West Ruislip and was worked to the relief cabin at Landor Street Junction by Saltley men, which was exceptionally handy for them, since their depot was situated just around the corner. Whilst the train was making its steady progress up through Buckinghamshire and Northamptonshire, the Derby men would be travelling passenger down to Birmingham New Street, where they would then change for the next local service to Duddeston, the closest station to Saltley. After a short walk through some decidedly dubious streets, the Derby driver and guard would finally reach the depot and make their presence known to the TCS, before continuing to the relief cabin. Eventually, the phone in the cabin would ring, informing them that their job was approaching. On arrival at Derby, the train would have to be propelled (reversed) under London Road Bridge and into the Carriage Works. Although the place had seen happier days, Litchurch Lane was still a vast site and was rumoured to have 365 sets of hand points, one for each day of the year. It was also a separate signing on the road card, so at this early stage in my career, I needed a conductor into the works, even though I had just worked the job from Birmingham and 4 Shed was less than 200 metres away.

Other unfitted work that occasionally came our way was the movement of preserved locomotives. These were transported to and from local preservation societies to the various depot open days around the region. Coalville and Leicester were always popular venues, and it was after one of these events when, along with a driver, I was tasked to return D100. *Sherwood Forester*, D8 *Penyghent* and the green-liveried Metrovick to Peak Rail at Matlock. Travelling passenger to Leicester, we made our way across to the depot where our train was waiting. However, my brakevan was missing two vital pieces of equipment. Before departure, I would first have to obtain some coal for the stove, as well as two old-fashioned paraffin side lamps. According to the Rule Book, the brakevan on an unfitted train had to display three red lights on a main line (i.e., a tail light and two side lights), and when on a goods line or loop, a white light must be displayed on the side adjacent to a running line. I was glad I'd paid attention the day they covered this at Toton. These lamps however, were virtually museum pieces and I have no idea where the Leicester TCS obtained a set, but it reinforces what I said earlier about certain practices not changing much from steam days. Fortunately, both lamps still had their interchangeable red lenses intact, and their paraffin reservoirs were full, so along with the electric tail light I already had, we were finally ready to depart.

Of course, during the trip from Leicester to Derby, we were switched between main line and goods line several times, so I was busy altering lenses for most of the journey. We also generated a bit of interest from the trainspotters on Derby station as we continued northbound. They were no doubt wondering why the guard was leaning out of the brakevan fiddling around with two paraffin lamps. At Ambergate station, the driver obtained the token, which gave us permission to proceed onto the Matlock Branch. I would also need it to operate the ground frame at Matlock station, which would allow entry into Peak Rail itself. The Matlock Branch is purely a passenger route and I had signed it as such, never really expecting to have to operate the ground frame, or carry out any intensive shunting operations there, some of which would have to take place on private property. It was another one of those instances where I had been told not to worry; I'd never have to go in there.

An important thing to remember, which could easily be overlooked in all the excitement, was that the train was unbraked. So, before anyone set about uncoupling the loco or brakevan, it was wise to apply at least one handbrake. The owner of the locos at Peak Rail had already witnessed one trainman, who had forgotten this small point, sprinting after his runaway locos. As soon as we arrived at Matlock, the heavens opened, and I got completely soaked in a matter of seconds. By the time I had figured out the ground frame and finished shunting, I was feeling rather miserable. Fortunately, I had maintained a nice fire in the brakevan and hung my clothes to dry as best as possible. The mash (tea) can had boiled and I enjoyed a nice hot cuppa on the way back down the branch to Derby. It felt like I had used all eight weeks of training in one day, but it had been a good learning experience. As we passed through Derby station for the second time that day, the trainspotters were no doubt wondering why a half naked guard was now flapping his clothes out of the brakevan.

The one steel job that Derby retained was the 12:11 Brierley Hill. It originated from the Eastern Region and was worked driver only operated (DOO) to Derby, for relief by a driver and guard. After progressing through Burton-upon-Trent and Tamworth, the train would be turned across at Water Orton, to cut through the seemingly endless expanse of Sutton Park. After negotiating Walsall, it would then continue along the South Staffordshire Line to the steel terminal at Brierley Hill. The job was essentially a trip working, where wagons were either picked up or dropped off at different sidings along the route. For instance, on its return from Brierley Hill, it would often be tasked to collect wagons from Round Oak and Wednesbury. Gaining access to Wednesbury Steel Terminal could be interesting at times. To enter the sidings, the train was required to propel, virtually blind, up a steep gradient. This wasn't always easy, particularly if you were trying to shove a heavy train on wet rails. With the loco (usually a Class 37) in reverse and the power handle wide open, the driver and guard would be desperately straining to see out of the cab windows, whilst the signalman in Wednesbury box would be shaking his head.

Derby Trainmen had an on-off relationship with postal trains. Sometimes the work seemed regular, then other times it disappeared from the links completely. When I first started at Derby, there was an afternoon job, which required a guard to travel passenger to Lincoln and work a parcels train back. The job itself was straightforward enough, but the guard would have to wait around at Lincoln for about four hours before his return working appeared. This wasn't necessarily a bad thing however, as a stroll around the shops, a meal, a visit to the Cathedral or even a pint or two could be most pleasant on a summer afternoon, before the rules regarding drinking on duty were strictly enforced – which tended to be after the derailment at Maidstone East on the 6th September 1993.

The Lincoln parcels seemed to vanish around the end of 1990 and there was no other postal work for trainmen until early 1993, when a late turn appeared. This time the guard, signing on at 21:22, would travel passenger to Birmingham New Street and work a travelling post office (TPO) train back. There would be around an hours' wait at Birmingham before the TPO arrived, then the post office staff would rush around it like ants, loading and unloading mail sacks before its next scheduled departure. Once this frenzied activity had died down a little, the postal workers would then begin sorting the mail in the carriages, whilst the guard checked the train and advised the driver of the load. After a brief scheduled stop at Burton-upon-Trent, where more mail sacks were hurriedly thrown off and on, the train would continue to Derby, arriving around midnight. The guard would return to 4 Shed, but with less than four hours on duty, he would have to sit spare in the mess room for a while, as the TCS was usually wise to any disappearing acts the trainman may have up his sleeve.

British Rail Research based at the Railway Technical Centre (RTC) in Derby provided a regular flow of work for 4 Shed. Along with track recording and gauging trains needing to be dragged here, there and everywhere, there were also periodic loco and rolling stock tests carried out at the Old Dalby test track in Leicestershire. This was the one and only road I avoided signing, simply because I found the work dull and repetitive in the extreme. If I had a preferred Research job, it was taking the track recording train (in transit) to Crewe, then returning by passenger train, or vice versa: nice and straightforward. Trains were prepared or stabled in the RTC sidings situated near Derby power signal box (PSB), and as most of these had to be propelled in and out, this place could be a difficult and exceptionally dangerous area to work in; a fact tragically demonstrated by the death of a shunter there one day.

Occasionally, the odd special working would come along and, in my short career at Derby, I got to work a steam special, a special charter using Orient Express stock and even the Royal Train, although the latter was merely an empty stock transit. There were also Officers' Specials, which involved dragging an observation carriage full of railway hierarchy around a certain area. These were often exaggerated affairs but could occasionally yield a bonus. They sometimes had their own chef aboard, so once the job was over, the train crew would be straight in to secure any leftovers. Another job I ended up with was preparing a train for use in a joint emergency exercise. Using condemned carriages, a spare truck from the fire brigade and several actors with made up injuries, a simulated rail accident was staged in Belper Goods Yard. The scenario was that a train had hit a lorry loaded with toxic chemicals and the resulting disaster would have to be dealt with by the three emergency services. Two mannequins played the part of the train crew, although, at times, it was difficult to tell which were which! The dummy driver was left in the cab, whilst the dummy secondman was unceremoniously thrown down the embankment, to be accounted for later. It never was, at least not until well after the event. The irony was not lost on me.

2. SITTING SPARE

Endless comings and goings, timesheets being filled in, the inevitable practical jokes, lively chatter punctuated with frequent shouts of "Who's mashing then?" (Making tea.) These were some of the activities that constituted life in 4 Shed mess room, and this was where you spent most of your time if you were booked spare. When I started at Derby, the only remnants of the original No 4 Shed were the locker room, stores, several offices accommodating the TCS, roster clerks and union staff, and the mess room itself. To be honest, the facilities were grim and would be considered unacceptable by today's standards, but the place was living history. Generations of enginemen had come and gone and only those walls remained to mark their passing and echo their shouts. When you were at 4 Shed, you really felt like another link in that historic chain, part of something larger and ultimately enduring.

The remnants of Derby 4 Shed in March 1992, which were demolished three months later. The mess room was situated to the far right. *Author*.

The nature of railway work demanded some rather unique hours of duty and the mess room essentially became like a second home. You can name any time on the 24-hour clock and I can safely say, as can most railway people, that over the years, I've signed on or off duty at all of them. 02:26, 14:43, 23:12, you saw the job at all times of the day and night, in all seasons, weathers and moods. Perhaps it's just the passing of time, but life seemed simpler then. There seemed much more freedom and light-heartedness, before the world went completely crazy. Spare men would sit outside during the long summer evenings; some would wash their car on a Sunday, if things were quiet. Darts, cards, gambling, pin-ups, fast cars, moderate drinking, all general bloke-type revelry, none of which was frowned upon because, at the time, you were a man in a man's world, and it was okay. The job got done and life made a lot of sense. Everything revolved around the simple pleasures of tea, tobacco, tall stories and the sharing of a common bond. If the mess room was like a second home, then many of the people became an extension of your family, simply because of the amount of time spent there.

The three most commonly used items in the mess room were the large communal teapot, the fruit machine, often referred to as the 'Bandit' and the hotline from the TCS to the mess room. This was situated on a shelf nearest the door. It would ring numerous times during a shift, primarily to inform relief crews that their trains were approaching or that the shed men were required, or that a job had just been found for one of the several unwilling bodies sitting spare. Occasionally, someone would lift the receiver and pretend they were talking to the TCS. Everyone would be too busy chatting to realize that the phone had never actually rung, so some unwitting individual would be dispatched on a fictitious errand, only to return later, rather red-faced.

Spare turns were an inevitable but necessary part of train crew rosters, giving management a flexible framework in which to allocate personnel. At most depots there were two shifts alternating between days and nights. You wouldn't normally see many people from the other shift, unless you had swapped turns with one of them or happened to be in the mess room during the crossover periods, i.e., midday or midnight. According to your current position in the link, you were either on a booked job or spare. If you were spare, the signing on time was often only a guide, as you could be moved two hours either side of it. For example, if you were 07:00 spare, you could be deemed fair game for any jobs that fell between 05:00 and 09:00, if the booked trainman didn't show, provided you signed the road of course. For the most part though, you would simply have to resign yourself to many a long hour in the mess room.

I was fortunate in some ways because I gained comprehensive road knowledge within a short space of time and could undertake most trainman jobs that came along. This kept my spare turns to a minimum, but even I began to succumb towards the end of 1992, when our work began to dry up. The only advantage to being spare was that after six hours, you could ask the TCS if he still required you. If he didn't, it was generally understood that you could go home and still get paid for eight hours. This goodwill worked both ways however, as you could be asked to stop and cover a job into overtime, if the need arose.

I found nights difficult at the best of times, but spare turns on nights were particularly soul-destroying. Some people preferred nights, but I always tried to swap mine for afternoon starts where possible, to remain with my own shift. Sometimes this wasn't possible, so I would have to endure a week of 22:00 spare or some other similar delight. During those dead hours, my stomach would grind away, not knowing if it wanted breakfast, lunch or tea, and the longer I sat in the mess room, the less I felt like doing anything. Invariably, you would end up with a job after about five hours, which was most unwanted. A typically irksome task that seemed to crop up regularly on nights was turning high speed train (HST) sets at Branston Junction. This job entailed taking the necessary HST set from Etches Park into the station. Once in the station, its second-class section would be leading (i.e., behind the lead power car as it heads towards London St. Pancras), and the purpose of the job was to ensure that the first-class section would be leading. This was achieved by using Branston, Birmingham Curve and Leicester Junctions, which formed a triangle just beyond Burton-upon-Trent. The work was undemanding enough, but after five hours, it was the last thing you wanted to do when your bed was almost within reach. The trainman would ride in the rear power car (first-class end) and stop the driver once clear of the shunt signal at Branston. He would then give the driver the buzzer code to set back and remain in that cab, ready to apply the emergency brake if necessary, as the driver propelled round to Birmingham Curve Junction. Once the driver was behind the main aspect there, he could proceed round to Leicester Junction and continue back to Derby. The trainman could join him up front but would usually remain in the back cab or the train itself. If the coaches hadn't been cleaned yet, he would probably be securing any booty. Newspapers and magazines were a favoured commodity during a long night in the mess room, but one of those well-travelled cheese sandwiches from the buffet car was best left alone. Incidentally, a mess room occupant could become extremely well read, with the variety of newspapers and periodicals from all around the country. As the HST pulled into Derby, its first-class section would now be leading, ready for its next departure to London. As St. Pancras is a terminus, all those hurried executive types travelling first-class would now be able to exit the station first as well, but I wonder how many of them appreciated it. It was just one of the many little jobs carried out during the early hours which made their world go round.

Being spare on days was more bearable, especially if there happened to be a good crowd in the mess room. Almost everyone took a turn at mashing in the communal teapot, so there was a brew on at least every hour. Practical jokes were virtually a way of life, and more importantly, helped to relieve much of the boredom. There were the usual gags of salt in the tea, which eventually progressed to chilli powder. Another favourite was exploding cigarettes and trainmen with plenty of time on their hands would usually manufacture one or two. Match head scrapings would be wrapped in silver foil and placed in the end of a cigarette. The cigarette would then be placed in a pack and left conveniently on the nearest table. Usually the gag was meant for a certain individual, but as railwaymen and magpies share a similar trait (i.e., petty theft), practically anyone could get caught. Sometimes the pack would be completely forgotten about, until a brief but unmistakable flaring up noise was heard, immediately followed by a startled curse. One habitual cigarette cadger, who always took the last one from a pack, then proceeded to compound his crime by emptying any loose tobacco flakes onto the nearest person's head, once fell victim to the mother of all exploding cigarettes. One day, he helped himself to a cigarette from the trainman's table as usual, but unbeknown to him, this one had been specially prepared. The devious mastermind who had arranged it obviously harboured some deep-seated grudge against the 'cadger' because this one contained a lot of match head scrapings. On the cadger's second drag, the cigarette flared up like a roman candle, conveniently removing all his nostril hair. He spent the rest of the day with a scorch mark on his upper lip, politely declining any further offers of cigarettes – an effective way to quit perhaps?

Each year, a small Christmas tree was set up in the mess room, but even this sacred symbol of peace and goodwill to all men wasn't exempt from use in practical jokes. After sitting for six hours, most spare men, on being given the TCS's permission to sign off, would quietly collect their things, bid their remaining colleagues a respectful farewell and quickly depart, but one trainman, on being given the 'right away' seemed to positively delight in rubbing his remaining colleagues' noses in it. Not content with this, he always wore large motorcycle gloves in winter (regardless that he'd never owned a motorcycle in his life) and had developed the rather unfortunate habit of whacking the person nearest the door over the head with them as he left. This was tolerated a couple of times, until one day he inadvertently left the offending items of clothing on the table whilst he went to obtain the TCS's permission to leave. His previous victims quickly filled the fingers of the oversized gloves with pine needles from the Christmas tree and waited for his return. It wasn't long before he came swaggering back into the mess room, making the usual comments about leaving his colleagues to do all the work. He then grabbed his gloves, smacked the nearest person around the head with them and departed. There were a few glorious seconds of silence then shouting could be heard outside, the nature of which seemed to relate to the alleged illegitimacy of the mess room's occupants. The gloves were targeted again soon after, when they were filled with water and placed in the freezer overnight. I believe he started wearing a less conspicuous pair and was more respectful on his departures after that.

Sometimes, if you sat in the mess room long enough, some unusual and challenging jobs would present themselves. I once had an unexpected trip to Immingham with a train of fuel tankers. Although it doesn't sound particularly thrilling, this was a real novelty for a trainman, as these jobs were normally driver only operated, and working to Immingham was virtually unheard of for Derby crew. It was also very nearly a one-way trip for me, although I didn't realize this until we were well under way. Owing to a malfunction, the Immingham driver had been forced to isolate the driver's safety device (DSD) in his cab, and according to the Rule Book, now required a secondman to ride with him. I was 14:00 spare and had been sitting for a couple of hours when I was given the job. The TCS assured me that I would be relieved at Nottingham, so armed with this knowledge, I happily boarded the Class 37, which awaited me on the goods line with its train of tankers. I greeted the Immingham driver, whom despite the day's mechanical problems seemed a pleasant enough chap.

As we approached Nottingham, the station appeared ominously devoid of people, especially those wearing train crew uniform, so we ground to a halt at the end of the platform and I phoned the signalman to check on the whereabouts of my supposed relief. The signalman at Trent PSB was almost as much an accomplished con man as my own TCS. He informed me that my relief was waiting at Lincoln, so on we went. I knew well before we even arrived at Lincoln that there was no relief scheduled. I was going the distance; it had just taken me a while to register the fact. It wouldn't have been so bad but getting home could be a problem. My Immingham colleague knew of no return working until the following morning, and it was very likely that by the time we reached our destination, I would have missed the last passenger train as well. As we rattled on through Newark, Lincoln and the 'dark territory' as I called it, either side of Market Rasen, the prospect of being stranded at Immingham began to sink in. This was developing into one of those legendary situations I had often heard about, but never actually thought would happen to me; the possibility of 24 hours' continuous duty. I would be joining the ranks of an elite few. At Wrawby Junction we joined the Cleethorpes line and continued towards Brocklesby Junction, where we were finally routed into Imminghan Dock. The air became thick and heavy with the sweet stench of petrochemicals and vast oil refineries lined each side of the track with their complicated network of pipes. A relief crew was waiting for us at the depot and I reported to the TCS, who confirmed my worst fears. I was in fact stranded, at least until morning.

I made myself as comfortable as possible in the unfamiliar mess room, whilst trying to come to terms with the long night that lay ahead of me. I had about six hours in at this stage, so by 05:00 first light, my total would be nearer fifteen. Add another three for the return journey and I'd be up to eighteen. This of course, was the best-case scenario. If there was no return working at 05:00, my total would rise still further. I was just contemplating this big payday, when the TCS suddenly appeared. Apparently, there was a job about to depart towards Cleethorpes, which was in the wrong direction as far as I was concerned, but I could 'bail out' at Habrough station, on the slim chance that the last passenger train hadn't yet gone. This was a gamble because if it had already departed, it would mean a cold night on the platform for me. There was a possibility of getting as far as Lincoln though, and as Immingham offered very little inducement to hang around, I boarded yet another Class 37 with a train of tankers and we snaked around Brocklesby Junction again towards Habrough. As soon as I set foot on the platform, I consulted the timetable, and much to my relief, the last passenger train was on its way. I'd made it with about five minutes to spare. I had gone from a potential 24-hour duty to a mere ten-hour shift, which was commonplace for me.

By sheer good fortune, this last Sprinter service was going all the way to Derby, and to my surprise, it was one of our drivers at the controls (I had forgotten that Derby still retained the Grimsby and Cleethorpes work.) I think the driver was more surprised than me because I was the last person he was expecting to see at such a dark and lonely outpost, so far from home. For my part, I was just glad to see a familiar face and be heading in the right direction. There were only a handful of passengers aboard who, according to the conductor guard, were all getting off at either Lincoln or Nottingham. This pleased the driver somewhat, as provided no one else wanted to get on, he could rattle through the numerous little stations on the route without stopping and possibly make last orders at his local. We slowed through every station, just to make sure no one was waiting, but otherwise hammered through the 'dark territory'. There was nothing out there except fields, farm crossings and the odd lonely signal box. We were just getting used to having the road in our favour and flying past all the green signals, when we were suddenly checked. The driver reduced speed accordingly and we were eventually brought to a stand at a red signal. It was an unusual place to be held, so on behalf of the driver I got straight on the phone. The signalman informed me that trains in both directions were being slowed, as apparently a patient from a nearby secure hospital had escaped and the police were searching for him at that very moment. I could see the foreboding building up on the hill with all its lights on. I could hear dogs barking and see torch beams sweeping back and forth. Suddenly, every tree and hedgerow harboured a madman waiting to pounce. Whilst my imagination was running riot, the signalman continued talking, but I wasn't listening. I was now feeling distinctly uncomfortable and was in a hurry to be off. It had all the elements of a classic horror film; a lunatic makes good his escape by assuming the identity of a humble trainman. But perhaps there were enough lunatic trainmen around already, so no one would really notice. I returned to the safety of the cab as quickly as possible and we proceeded at caution for the next 200 metres or so before the driver opened up again. There was a pint somewhere with his name on it, or so he kept telling me. After negotiating Lincoln and Nottingham, we finally pulled into Derby and it was one weary trainman, with a few more grey hairs, who returned to 4 Shed that night.

A vital, but often overlooked aspect of any job was the run round manoeuvre. This involved getting a train to face in the desired direction by means of uncoupling the loco from one end and re-coupling it to the other. Whether carried out in some far-flung corner of the network or simply in the station yard, it was usually the trainman's responsibility. Allied with this duty came the brake continuity test, which had to be carried out whenever a loco was coupled to a train or other vehicles coupled or uncoupled. It didn't matter if the train was vacuum or air braked; the principle was essentially the same. After the trainman had hooked on the coupling and connected the necessary brake pipes, the driver would then begin charging up the system, which would gradually release the train brakes. Whilst this was taking place, the trainman would walk to the end and put a tail lamp on the last wagon. Once the system was fully charged, he could then open the air cock, or disconnect the vacuum pipe on the last wagon. This exhausted the air, or destroyed the vacuum in the system, thus breaking the continuity and causing all the train brakes to re-apply. After checking the last three wagon brakes had functioned correctly (by kicking the blocks), the trainman would close the air cock, or replace the vacuum pipe and the driver would recharge the system again. On satisfactory completion of the test, the train would be deemed fit to proceed.

Because of accidents or engineering work, numerous freight jobs could be diverted via Derby, with some requiring to be run round in the station yard. It was on these occasions when a spare trainman would be called upon to undertake this duty and dispatch the various jobs on their onward journeys. The most memorable one I did was perhaps the Lakenby-Corby steel coil train (the heaviest regular freight service), one grey, showery day. Each coil weighed in at about 25 tonnes (or so I was told), with a pair of Class 37s pulling a gross train weight of around 2,200 tonnes. As I proceeded towards the end of the train to perform the brake test, I became aware of a definite increase in ambient temperature and an intermittent hissing noise. At first, I thought there must be some problem with the wagons, until I realized the coils were fresh from the finishing mill. Although outwardly they didn't look hot, they were still radiating intense heat and the intermittent hiss was the sound of raindrops hitting their surface and evaporating. I found out later that hot rolled coil (HRC) could be loaded straight onto the wagons at temperatures of up to 500 degrees centigrade!

Not all run round jobs came uninvited and my one-off trip to Immingham wasn't Derby's only involvement with petroleum tanks. The Economac Oil Siding at Derby St. Andrews had frequent deliveries of petroleum products from various refineries and it was normally the spare trainman's job to run the train round in the station yard, or Derby North, before it was propelled into the siding. Most propelling movements into sidings were hazardous, but Economac was especially so. The track was curved and the driver unable to see any hand signals, so several rules had to be broken to successfully position trains in there. As had happened in so many sidings before, the person giving the hand signals could easily slip under the train and the driver would be completely unaware. With that in mind, I always adopted the procedure of standing well clear whilst the driver set back slowly. Once the train had been roughly positioned at the terminal, I would then partially dump the brake from the last wagon and stop him. It wasn't the most glamorous method, but it was certainly the safest.

Another less frequent job was the delivery of aviation fuel for the jet engine test beds at Rolls-Royce. After being run round, this train would have to be taken along the Sinfin Branch to its discharge point at Sinfin Central. The branch was accessed at Melbourne Junction, just over a mile southwest of Derby. As well as the Rolls-Royce siding, there were also two small stations, and three ground frames to contend with. No1 and No2 frames operated the run round loop, whilst No3 frame controlled the trap points adjacent the siding. After operating No3 frame, a loaded train could be propelled straight into the siding. Rolls-Royce emptied the tanks as required, so the loco would either return to its home depot or lay over at 4 Shed. Eventually the tanks would be discharged and a loco would be dispatched to collect them. This time, the accompanying trainman would have to employ all three frames, as once clear of the siding, the train would be propelled into the loop and the loco run round. Back in the station yard, it may have to be run round again, depending on its destination.

In the absence of proper conductor guards at the station, spare trainmen were sometimes called upon to work passenger trains. Although I considered myself a freight guard through and through, working the occasional passenger train did offer some variety. One day you might be working a HST from Sheffield to London, the next, a Sprinter to Matlock, Nottingham or Crewe. We didn't issue tickets, collect any money or really have much interaction with the passengers at all. We were there merely to operate the trains safely and in accordance with the Rule Book. To act as a passenger guard, trainmen still had to have the necessary road knowledge for a job, but also required additional training on HSTs, Sprinters and coaching stock, or slam-door stock as it was often referred to.

In due course, trainmen received a days' instruction on each common class of Sprinter unit (Classes 150-158) and a day each on coaching stock, diesel multiple units (DMU) and HSTs. The training involved basic things such as preparation, fault-finding, emergency procedures and the operation of the automatic doors on the new Sprinter units. Emergency coupling was also covered, although this applied primarily to HSTs. These had two emergency couplings in each power car; one was a fixed bar for coupling two HST sets together, the other was shorter with a pivoted head for HST to loco coupling. We were given a traction manual to study beforehand, in which the coupling diagrams were notoriously difficult to follow, but after a practical demonstration, they really became self-explanatory. Provided the HST towing eye had been fully extended and all the necessary locking pins were in place, the hardest part was probably getting the loco hook at the correct distance from the pivoted end of the bar, for it to be offered up and secured. Obviously, you couldn't stand between the buffers to facilitate this operation, so it took a few shunts to get exactly right. After that, it was simply a case of connecting the air pipes and any electrics, then performing a brake test. This would be achieved by pushing the emergency brake plunger in the cab of the rear power car.

We were told that it wouldn't really be our job anyway, because in most cases there would be a senior conductor aboard and it was their responsibility to prepare the emergency coupling. We were also told that one day pigs would achieve flight. The standard excuse always offered by 'senior condoms' keen to avoid this particular duty, was that their £200 company issue suit would get dirty. That they were issued with overalls, as well as dry cleaning tokens, didn't seem to have any bearing on the matter.

When a group of us learnt HSTs, we practised putting on the two different couplings in the sidings, never really expecting to have to do it for real. In fact, I think most trainmen probably went their whole career without having to do it, but I ended up doing it several times during the winter of 1991. That was the year we had the 'wrong kind of snow'. It may have been an unfortunate statement from a public relations point of view, but not altogether an incorrect one. It *was* the wrong kind of snow, compared to what we usually had. This stuff was unnaturally dry and powdery, almost like sand. It would barely stick together when compressed but had an amazing ability to funnel into the engine compartments of HSTs and literally clog everything up. I'd certainly never encountered snow like this before and the HSTs seemed to be suffering because of it.

There was one day in February when it seemed like the entire HST fleet was succumbing to this unusual weather. I had originally signed on duty at 12:22 for the Denby job, but as it was cancelled, I ended up sitting spare. I didn't have to sit around for long though because I was immediately dispatched with a driver to go and rescue a failed HST near Moorthorpe station. This was a London-Newcastle service, which had already encountered problems with the snow and had now apparently given up completely. As there were still passengers on board we would have to work the service to Leeds, where it would be terminated. After being allocated a Class 47, we departed light loco from 4 Shed and proceeded rapidly north through Chesterfield, Sheffield and Rotherham, before being crossed over just before Bolton-on-Dearne station. This enabled us to bypass the failed train and continue towards West Kirby Junction, where we were crossed back over, then given permission to proceed into the occupied section towards it. As expected, the senior conductor hadn't prepared the coupling, or even carried out any detonator protection, and stood there looking rather useless in his £200 suit. This was not a good start as far as I was concerned. I climbed into the guard's compartment of the lead power car and removed the access panel where the emergency couplings were stored...only to find none there. I would now have to trudge all the way down to the rear power car, in the hope that its set would be intact. I was beginning to feel a little frustrated, as I stumbled down the ballast with 200 pairs of passengers' eyes glaring at me. Why had this train been allowed to enter service with vital equipment missing? Why was the senior conductor unable to do his job properly? As I climbed into the rear power car, I noticed a passenger waiting at the guard's door. I knew he was about to make some enquiry regarding the train's delay, but as I wasn't in the best of moods at that moment, I pretended not to see him. That way, I wouldn't have to waste time answering foolish questions. Instead, I concentrated on removing the access panel with my T-key. Unfortunately, all the square keyholes had been rounded off, rendering my key completely useless. As I struggled to get my fingertips behind the panel, I made the mistake of glancing over my shoulder at the passenger. He was just about to open his mouth, when rage suddenly overtook me. I tore the six-foot panel off with my bare hands and threw it to the floor then turned to him with what must have been a face like thunder. Whatever question he was about to ask, he thought better of it and scuttled back to his seat. Still seething, I grabbed the HST to loco coupling, hoisted its near 30kg weight onto my shoulder and speed marched to the other end. By the time I got there, the physical exertion had provided an adequate outlet for my anger and I was able to couple up without further delay.   I did consider grabbing the senior conductor by his lapels and giving him a vigorous shake, but instead, gritted my teeth and returned to the rear power car to perform a brake test.

We were finally able to depart Moorthorpe and I resumed my role as secondman, whilst the senior conductor attended to his duties in the train, whatever they were.   We then had a brief stop at Wakefield before terminating at Leeds. At least for the HST, it was only a short trip from there to the depot at Neville Hill for attention, but for the remaining passengers, it was probably going to be a much longer journey. We were uncoupled by the station shunter and signalled into a vacant siding to await further instructions. My driver however, had other ideas and requested an alternative destination just around the corner, which became my one and only visit to Holbeck. Whether we sat in the official mess room or not, I don't know, but it certainly wasn't what I was expecting. It was more like someone's front room circa 1920s and there was a distinct *Mary Celeste* feel about it.   There was a kettle on the boil and a couple of vacant armchairs in front of a glowing coal fire. On an adjacent wall, a pendulum clock kept time with its constant but compelling beat. The place was empty apart from a cat, which gave us a questioning glance before returning to its slumbers in front of the fire. Spare men at 4 Shed often joked about who would end up as the mess room cat, but now I had met the official, undisputed one, albeit at Holbeck. It was now almost dark outside, and the only thing required to complete the effect would have been candles or gaslights. It was certainly a cosy environment in which to enjoy a cuppa, but it was all very surreal and would have made an excellent episode of the *Twilight Zone*.

We were returned to the present rather abruptly when the phone rang and a distant voice on the other end instructed us to proceed to Neville Hill. After negotiating our way into the depot, it turned out that we would be returning to Etches Park with yet another failed HST. As we were eager to get under way as soon as possible, I coupled up loco to HST for the second time that day and carried out a brake test, before obtaining permission to depart. The journey home was uneventful and on arrival at Derby, we dragged the snowbound HST onto a vacant stabling road near Etches Park and returned light loco to the shed. I was expecting my other crew members from our cancelled Denby job to be long gone by now, but it turned out that they had spent their afternoon and early evening rescuing HSTs as well.

By the summer of 1992, a permanent pre-fabricated building had been erected on part of the car park and the remaining bit of 4 Shed demolished. The reasonably happy, settled period I had come to know was essentially over. Major changes were taking place and they weren't all for the best. It was the beginning of the end when we moved into that new mess room and I knew it. The old ways were dead, and I didn't like this humourless, sterile, politically correct way of working at all. As Derby lost more and more freight work, the true reality of sitting spare became painfully apparent.

Apart from the continuing practical jokes and general tomfoolery to curb the boredom, the only real laugh I remember having in the new mess room was when about eight trainmen, myself included, were booked 08:00 spare. At 14:00, we were all anxious to get home, but no one had quite plucked up the courage to ask the senior TCS if they could go yet. If one was allowed home, then by rights, all the 08:00 spare men could go, but no one wanted to be the first to ask; everyone was waiting for everyone else. Also, there were a lot of us and it would be a trifle indiscreet if we all went tramping out together, firing up our respective vehicles in the car park. (Trainmen were renowned for their old bangers, as opposed to the drivers in their sleek, high-powered models.) Eventually, someone decided to chance their luck and made their way along the corridor from the mess room to the TCS' office. Not wanting to miss any favourable response from the TCS, the other trainmen waited in the corridor or pretended to read the notice boards in the lobby. As soon as the TCS gave the nod to this one individual, it was like a scene from *The Great Escape*. The signal was relayed from the trainmen in the lobby to the many bodies waiting in the corridor, all with their bags and coats at the ready. It was an immediate mass exodus and the TCS could only stare in shock as we all trooped out. I think he had to check if there was anyone still in the mess room after we'd all gone. There was so much exhaust from all the cars starting simultaneously, that the shed men appeared, thinking someone had just arrived with a rake of Class 31s. These locos were not known for their environmental friendliness. With the demise of Class 20s, several pairs of 31s were regularly stabled at 4 Shed. Usually they were left idling, but when started from cold, they belched out a thick fog of choking diesel fumes, so much so, that the station would not be visible from 4 Shed for several minutes.

3. SHED MEN

The phone would ring then the same inevitable cry of "Shed Men!" would issue around the mess room. Usually, you'd just started a meal, perhaps got into a newspaper or TV programme or simply got your head down. Either way, the timing was always inconvenient, even if you were doing nothing, which was usually the case. Generally, the shed job was the best one to have. By that, I mean it was marginally better than sitting spare because at least you had some suggestion of usefulness to justify your presence in the mess room and there was less danger of being sent off on some dodgy job. You also roughly knew the amount of work involved and could generally guarantee a finishing time. The other bonus was that rarely did you venture any further than station limits – although absolutely none of this could be relied upon.

I can count on one hand the amount of times I got the shed job at the weekend, but I considered myself fortunate if it was my booked turn or I happened upon it by chance, because it meant missing out on any dubious ballast workings. Unless something drastic happened, I knew I could disappear after about six hours, whereas ballast crews could be stuck in the middle of nowhere, often for unknown lengths of time (see Chap. 5). Initially the signing on times for shed were the standard 06:00, 14:00 and 22:00 shifts, and each turn could involve more than fifteen loco preparations and disposals, as well as other maintenance related tasks. In 1992, the signing on times were changed to 08:00, 16:00 and 00:05, for reasons I never really understood. The job was adequately covered throughout the 24-hour period, so why change a regular shift pattern to an irregular one? I felt that it was done to make the job slightly less palatable and to further unsettle the workforce, but conspiracy theories weren't as popular then as they are now.

Once a loco arrived on shed, it would be left outside the fuelling point, a place commonly referred to as the 'Wind Tunnel'. The TCS would then summon his shed men, and after a polite pause, the designated driver and trainman would trudge dutifully around to his office to receive instructions regarding the stabling of the loco. The roads primarily associated with shed moves consisted of the front and back roads through the wind tunnel, which were accessed through spring points permanently set in that direction. Next to the wind tunnel lay shed side, after which came three roads designated N3, N2 and N1 respectively. N3 was a through road and remained clear, whilst N2 and N1 were both stabling roads. Locos would arrive at various times throughout the 24-hour period, although the hours between 20:00 and 02:00 often generated the most activity. After consulting with the fitters (Mechanical & Electrical Engineers), the shed men would move the loco into the wind tunnel and shut it down, ready to receive fuel and water. Minor defects could be rectified at this stage, but if something more complex was required, or if the loco was scheduled an 'A' exam, it would be moved onto the front road for further attention.

Sometimes arriving locos would need to bypass the wind tunnel altogether and this was one of the occasions where the trainman would have to hold the spring points across whilst the driver carried out the move. Whenever I operated those points, there was always the fear in the back of my mind about momentarily losing grip of the lever after the lead bogie had passed over, thus causing the rear bogie to head towards the wind tunnel, the result being a complete obstruction of the shed access. Fortunately, it never happened to me, but it was certainly one way to stop the job.

Whilst fuelling and watering, the fitters would also clean the cab windows, headlights and marker lights. On completion, the shed men would restart the loco and continue through the wind tunnel and out over the N road head points. As the driver changed ends, the trainman would pull the necessary hand points for the desired stabling road. If there was a lengthy period before its next duty, the loco would be shut down and its battery isolation switch (BIS) taken out. Otherwise it would be left running, but in either case, its handbrake would be applied. During the night, HST sets also came through the wind tunnel for fuel and water before returning to Etches Park Carriage Sidings via the station. No trainmen were required for this job, as there weren't many hand points to pull. Nevertheless, the shed at night could become a hive of activity in a short space of time.

In theory, any driver could end up on shed, but most of the time a trainman would be paired up with a driver whom, for medical reasons, had been restricted to station limits or jobs which always involved a secondman. Regular characters included the likes of Driver Welsh, Big Bill and Harry C., which often set the stage for many hours of light-hearted entertainment. As a new, inexperienced trainman it did take a while to learn the ropes and get used to certain drivers' idiosyncrasies. Some viewed you with complete contempt, whilst others couldn't do enough for you, but I found even the most cantankerous ones came around in the end, given enough time. With locos waiting to be moved, and more coming onto the shed all the time, it made sense to share the driving duties. Trust was the key element, but this obviously took a while to earn. Some drivers explained the locos to you, showed you the necessary procedures and even let you drive under their supervision, so eventually you became experienced and trusted enough to move them on your own. The first loco I drove under such supervision was 47973 *Derby Evening Telegraph,* which for a young trainman just starting out, was a real thrill. It was also quite fitting, as it had been the *Derby Evening Telegraph*, in late 1989, where I had seen Trainman (D) vacancies advertised; a vacancy I had applied for and subsequently come to occupy. Even though the rules were severely stretched by allowing trainmen to drive, it was generally accepted as common practice and the only sensible way to get the job done. We were supposed to be future drivers after all. In time, many drivers were happy to lend you their key and remain in the mess room whilst you dealt with the locos, only to grudgingly appear if things suddenly became hectic.

It took me a lot longer to acquire the much sought-after drivers' key though, and I only got one in the end because Harry C. became fed up of me constantly borrowing his. Nevertheless, I now had a key of my own and was able to operate on the shed effectively and with confidence.

I always enjoyed dealing with Class 20s whenever they appeared. Their cabs may have been a bit spartan and uncomfortable, and they were certainly showing their age by the early 1990s, but I found them to be good, solid, reliable workhorses with a unique character – not to mention a most agreeable engine sound. They were still the common traction on most of the Derby ballast jobs, being employed primarily on weekend engineering trains and trip workings, as well as the Chadd' Shunt, and of course the Denby coal trains. They also had a passenger turn in the summer holidays, hauling the 'Jolly Fisherman' to Skegness, although by the beginning of 1992, their appearances were unfortunately becoming less frequent. If there happened to be a pair of them in the wind tunnel, I would always commandeer them first, leaving a grumbling Harry C. to deal with any other locos behind. Once the fitter had given the all clear, I would unlock the driving desk, move the controller from the 'off' position to 'engine only', letting it prime for a few seconds before pressing the start button and revelling in the throaty roar of the twin locos. The fitter would take cover as thick, acrid exhaust plumes filled the wind tunnel, then I would release the handbrake, energize the automatic warning system (AWS), un-peg the train brake, move the controller into the 'forward' position, and finally, with one foot on the DSD pedal, release the straight air brake. Although it was bad practice, I just couldn't resist pulling the power handle wide open in one move. At first nothing would happen, then there would be an ominous click as the relays kicked in. Within seconds, the engine noise would change from a passive tick over to that distinctive high-pitched cylinder thump, and then...lift off! I guess it was the railway equivalent of launching an F-14 Tomcat from an aircraft carrier. With stereo sound, I would power out of the wind tunnel, only to shut off rather quickly to negotiate the points outside. If the power handle was shut off too sharply, there would be an unpleasant thump and a rather disturbing blue flash from the control cubicle (traction motor contacts), so the trick was to close the power handle to notch one, then allow the engines to power down before shutting off fully. If you planned it properly, you could coast happily right out over the head points, change ends, then set the other hand points for your required stabling road...pure magic! Stabling the locos was simply a reversal of the start up procedure, but if they were to be shut down, the BIS would have to be taken out on both locos, as well as the lighting switch. These were located outside between the bogies and resembled something from a Frankenstein film; big folding lever switches that sometimes emitted a spark to the unwary. When preparing Class 20s, I couldn't resist quoting the famous line "It's Alive!" as I re-engaged their BISs.

Class 47s were another favourite of mine and represented a good proportion of our shed work. They would arrive from all over the country, requiring attention after a hard day's labour. Although I was brought up with the traditional BR blue livery, I thought the new InterCity colours looked particularly smart. To see the wind tunnel at night occupied exclusively by InterCity 47s was an impressive sight. I found them fascinating; where had they come from? What trains had they hauled? What sights had they seen along the way? I don't think there were many people who shared such a romantic view of them, but it was difficult not to like such a faithful class of locomotive and attribute some sort of personality to them. It was quite easy really, especially when they were taking on water. Once their header tank was full, and without any regard to nearby personnel, they would blow the excess water through an overflow valve in their roof, just like a whale. The fitter would receive a cold shower if he was close, but it was almost as if the loco was trying to say "I've had a long hard day and I'm tired. Turn that bloody hose off and put me to bed!" I could see how Rev. Awdry had got some of his ideas. Human beings built these machines after all, why shouldn't they display some of our characteristics?

I don't know how much of an enthusiast Harry C. was of Class 47s, because he fell victim to at least two humorous misfortunes with them on shed. The first happened when he and his trainman were tasked to move a pair of 47s from shed side. Quite logically, he dispatched his younger mate to the rear loco, whilst he climbed up into the other one. Obviously, the plan was to drive off in opposite directions, but unfortunately, neither of them had realized the locos were coupled together. By amazing coincidence, they both opened their power handles at the same time, only to find themselves in a tug of war contest. Instead of a rope, it was two straining 47s. Realizing there was a fault, Harry shut off first, and as the coupling went slack, his loco ricocheted off the buffers of the other one several times. This caused him to lean out of the cab window and utter his usual catchphrase, which contained two expletives far too colourful to print here. The second occasion involved the classic engine shutdown prank. Harry would start up a 47, but unbeknown to him, his shed mate would sneak into the back cab and shut it down. A now concerned Harry would restart the engine, only for it to shut down again after a few seconds. Grumbling to himself, he would disappear into the engine room with his hand lamp to investigate the circuit breakers before returning for a restart. By this time, his mate had sensibly vacated the back cab, because instead of colourful expletives, he would probably end up with a clip round the ear. Harry would finally get under way, no doubt still grumbling to himself about awkward locos.

Preparing and disposing of locos was the responsibility of the driver, as trainmen were not deemed to possess the necessary technical knowledge until they had completed their MP12 (driving) course. However, by observing the process often enough, I was able to do a basic loco preparation in an emergency, or rather, if my driver had dodged off somewhere. Such disappearances could be common, often involving a woman or last orders, but sometimes both. After walking around the loco and checking its pipes, bogies, lights and any external gauges, it would be up into the cab to establish the status of the safety equipment. This involved flags, detonators, track circuit clips and fire extinguishers. Fuel and water gauges would be checked next in the engine room, along with the circuit breakers. After engaging the BIS, the engine would be started, and the correct air pressures observed, before performing brake, power, DSD and electric train supply (ETS) tests. It would then be a trip through the engine room, to conduct the same tests in the other cab. If you were conscientious, both cabs could be swept clean as well.

Sometimes locos would need to be coupled together and this is where the trainman came into his own area of expertise. Donning his oily, full length orange smock and gloves, he would squeeze under the buffers, hook the coupling on and connect all the various pipes. Class 47s were straightforward enough, but Class 20s and 31s could have six different connections, including the vacuum pipe and the extremely awkward jumper cable, which often had to be knocked in or out of its socket with a brick. With all these pipes, space between the locos was at a premium, and as a result, there weren't too many overweight trainmen on the job.

Another duty of the shed men was to take Class 47s to Etches Park for replacement brake blocks. It was one of those jobs that sounded straightforward enough but could turn into quite an excursion at times. Once beyond the head points for the N roads, the loco would continue past the carriage sidings and into the shunt neck alongside the maintenance shed. Whilst the driver changed ends, the trainman would get the necessary clearance from the maintenance supervisor. Safety rules dictated that the supervisor had to warn his staff of any loco movements in the shed. This was achieved by him activating a series of blue flashing lights above the designated road, in conjunction with an audible warning; in this case, a two-tone siren. He had plenty of time to get his safety measures in place because to get the loco from the shunt neck to the front of the shed, the trainman may have to pull as many as eight different sets of hand points, whilst also keeping a good lookout for HSTs and any other conflicting shunt movements, not to mention the multitude of trip hazards that littered the carriage sidings. Finally, the loco would be on the correct road facing the shed and the driver would change ends again, ready to drive in once the large roller shutter door opened. When it did, it was like entering the shuttle bay of the Starship *Enterprise;* flashing lights, sirens and men in boiler suits looking busy. For the fitters to comfortably attend the bogies, the shed floor was roughly four foot below rail height, so once the loco was safely inside, there was a good ten-foot drop for the train crew to overcome. The supervisor was most adept at operating his disco lights but when it came to appearing with a set of portable steps, his record was not so good. The sight of Big Bill hanging from the loco handrails at full extent, his legs flailing in mid-air, was not a pretty one, so the often younger, more agile trainman would perform the aerial acrobatics and eventually commandeer some steps. Re-blocking a loco could be a lengthy process, so the shed men would walk back to 4 Shed mess room, to await their next call.

4. SHUNT & TRIP

T89 – The Chadd' Shunt

To receive the full trainman salary, new starters were encouraged to sign for their first road as soon as possible, and Chaddesden Sidings was usually it. Situated towards the north end of the station and around Chadd' curve, eight roads constituted the Civil Engineers (CE) tip sidings, shared in part with Steetley Construction Materials. Just to confuse things however, the through roads were numbered 2 to 7, with a dead-end cripple road in between designated 6a. (There was also an outside road, separate from the main body of the sidings.) As a full train crew was required for this job (i.e., a driver, secondman and guard), a novice trainman could act as secondman and learn the ropes reasonably quickly, usually signing for the job within a matter of days.

A pair of Class 20s was the usual form of traction, but these stalwart locos were eventually replaced with a single Class 31, which just didn't have the same appeal to me. After signing on at 07:15, the crew would depart light loco from 4 Shed and, on the brief journey through the station yard, would pass Slums Sidings and its associated Engine Sidings ground frame on the right. Signing for Chadd' also included this little enclave, but on querying the frame with the other crew members, the standard response was elicited, "Don't worry, you'll never have to go in there." To be fair, I only had to go into Slums Sidings about three times in four years, so I guess they were partly right.

At least four roads at Chadd' were always occupied with ZCV (Clam) ballast wagons, so unless an empty road had been left preset, the guard would have to pull the necessary hand points for the loco to proceed to the shunters' cabin at the far end of the sidings. There were at least two shunting staff permanently based there, and after consulting with them about forthcoming operations, work would either commence in earnest, or everyone would retire for a cuppa. It was invariably the latter.

The CE department was charged with the repair and maintenance of the railway infrastructure, with most of this work being carried out at the weekends, (see Chap. 5). Engineering (or departmental) trains would arrive at Chadd' on Sunday, loaded with spoil from various weekend worksites. These wagons would be unloaded during the week, with the spoil being reclaimed or dumped in the adjacent gravel pits as landfill. By this time, the shunting staff would have received the weekly ballast circular detailing train requirements for the following weekend, so trains would be continually marshalled at Chadd' and other CE sidings, to meet these requirements. Trains would be set for unloading, empty wagons would need to be marshalled into trains to collect fresh ballast, wagons containing fresh ballast would have to be marshalled into weekend engineering trains as required, whilst crippled wagons would be shunted out accordingly. These were all typical duties carried out by the T89 loco and crew.

Saturday was usually the busiest day for shunting, as last-minute wagon changes, or even the complete re-marshalling of some trains might be required, before they all began disappearing to their respective worksites from early evening onwards. The guard was sometimes called upon to assist, but if there were two shunters present, they knew where they wanted things and normally conducted operations on the ground whilst the train crew remained in the cab. Things were more efficient that way, and besides, it was helpful to have as many eyes in the cab as possible once the shunting got under way.

To facilitate operations, most wagons were loose shunted, which meant the continuous train brake generated by the loco was not used. Wagons to be shunted from the train would be uncoupled and have the vacuum (or air) drained from their brake reservoirs, then once the loco had provided enough momentum, the idea was for them to roll towards their allotted roads by themselves. As there were no brake pipes to worry about, this enabled the shunting staff to couple or uncouple portions of the train using a shunting pole, which saved them from having to scramble under the buffers each time.

This vital but unassuming piece of equipment was a wooden pole about eight feet in length with a metal hook (pig's tail) at one end. To uncouple, the shunter would rest the pole on a buffer sleeve and position one end underneath the coupling. Using the sleeve as a fulcrum, he would then push downwards and flick the coupling off its draw hook. Coupling up required a little more skill and involved catching the dangling coupling with the pig's tail and flicking it up onto the draw hook, again using the buffer sleeve for leverage if required. To have any success with the shunting pole, the couplings would have to be slack and the buffers compressed, so the train would often still be in motion whilst these operations were carried out – which is why the pole was eight feet long and the shunter remained well clear of the buffers. The brake stick was a more substantial piece of wood, rather like a squared off baseball bat. It had a million and one uses, but not all of them were legal, or even railway orientated. Nevertheless, its primary function in life was to aid in the application or release of wagon handbrakes. Using the brake stick to force down handbrake levers and secure them with their locking pin was the prescribed method of applying handbrakes, whereas pulling the pin whilst simultaneously giving the lever a smack with the brake stick, was the most effective way to release them. It could be quite a stress-busting experience, walking the length of the train knocking off handbrakes.

Shunting wagons is a real art, and with the right crew all working as one, it could almost be like poetry in motion. Shunting with a pair of Class 20s was an unrivalled experience though, and it wasn't usually long before wagons were flying everywhere...sometimes literally! The loco would be coupled to a long string of unsorted wagons and the whole train would then have to set back around Chadd' curve, almost into the station yard, to clear the sidings head points. All shunting movements were controlled by hand signal, and with a train nearly half a mile in length, it could be difficult to see the shunter at times, but once clear of the head points, he would raise both his arms indicating us to stop. There would be a brief pause whilst he set the required road and used his shunting pole to uncouple a portion of the train before calling us forward. As the uncoupled portion had to be given enough momentum to proceed towards its allotted road on its own, his hand signal would become more vigorous if we weren't pushing quickly enough. In this case, the driver would open the power handle fully. At first there would be no response, then the engines would rapidly power up, increasing in noise and speed. Within seconds, the shunter would raise both his arms again and the driver would quickly close the power handle, whilst simultaneously applying the loco brake. There would be the characteristic dull thump as the engines powered down, as well as the occasional blue flash from the control cubicle. The loco would initially come to a dead stand, but then the remaining wagon couplings would stretch out, hurling it another couple of feet. Anything not properly secured or wedged, including the guard and the teapot, would be thrown forward and the uncoupled portion of the train would be observed (hopefully) rolling towards its desired road, with the other shunter in hot pursuit. To retard and ultimately halt its motion, he would have to jam his brake stick under the nearest wagon leaf spring, using it as a fulcrum to press down on the handbrake lever with his full weight. 'Riding the brake stick' was a dangerous practice and strictly against the rules, as it could easily snap, sending the unfortunate operative under the wheels. Nevertheless, once the wagons had been positioned satisfactorily, the shunter would signal the driver to set back again to repeat the procedure. In this way, a long string of wagons would be sorted, crippled wagons removed (or created) and individual trains marshalled on their designated roads.

If only one shunter was available, he would continue to work his magic with the shunting pole whilst the guard operated the hand points as required. The shunter would shout which road to set for the next move, so it was imperative for the guard to remember how the roads were numbered. It was all very well standing at the head points and hearing the shunter shout 7, but if you counted across from 1 to 7 and forgot to include 6a in your calculations, then the result could be devastating, particularly since 6a had buffer stops about half way along it. This was probably the easiest way to slip up, but with loose shunting there were other, less obvious ways. Once when I was the secondman, we had just sent a raft of six wagons down one road, when the shunter called a halt for a tea break. Thinking these wagons would have their motion arrested by the already stationary wagons on that road, we trundled past them on an adjacent empty road to the cabin. All the through roads converged near the cabin and we sat there waiting for the pot to boil. As I was reaching for my cup, I just happened to glance out of the side window and saw a long string of wagons heading straight for us. The loose wagons had collided with the stationary ones, which obviously hadn't been secured properly because they were now all heading our way. There was no time to do anything as they were already on top of us, so I simply told my driver to hold onto something as we were about to be hit. Thinking I was joking, he laughed, but in the next second, there was an almighty crash and he was literally thrown from his chair. The wagons were perhaps only travelling about 5mph, but they hit us with a force of several tonnes. The impact caused the last two wagons to become derailed, but fortunately the damage to the loco was minimal and the only injury sustained was one of the driver's more sensitive areas being scalded with tea.

Although Chadd' prepared many of the trains used in the repair and maintenance of the region's tracks, its own sidings left a lot to be desired. Most of its tracks and points were in a poor state, and with a combination of wooden sleepers and loose chairs, it made the roads especially prone to spreading. This is when the rails are pushed wider apart and the wagon or loco wheels fall between them, causing the train to become derailed. Much as it might come as a surprise to the Railway Inspectorate or some health and safety statistician, having wagons off the road at Chadd' was commonplace, but often easily remedied amongst ourselves without involving any paperwork. More than once, one of the resident mechanical shovels was employed to re-rail errant wagons. However, on one occasion the loco itself became derailed and the breakdown crane had to be sent for, so there was no avoiding the subsequent 'Please Explain' forms.

Even though most of its work was carried out in the sidings, T89 was still classed as a trip working and sometimes had to venture out into the wider world, usually to collect or deliver wagons as required. A regular destination was Sandiacre Ballast Sidings situated in Toton yard. If a train had to be taken there, it would no doubt be marshalled during the morning, and once shunting had ceased for the day, the guard would couple the loco to it. Walking down one side, he would then check couplings and handbrakes before placing a tail lamp on the last wagon and performing a brake test. The checks would be repeated up the other side of the train, and once back at the loco, a driver's slip would have to be made out. Whenever a loco was coupled to its train for the first time, or a train's configuration altered en-route (i.e., loaded, unloaded or shunted), a driver's slip would be required for its on-going journey. This was where the guard had to complete a standard form detailing the characteristics of his train, matched against the route it would be taking. Limits for a route would be obtained from a freight loads book and entered on the left (authorised) side of the slip. The guard would then have to consult his Working Manual (white pages) or the information table painted on each wagon, to calculate his train's length, weight, speed and brake force, before entering them on the right (actual) side of the slip. Provided the figures in the actual column didn't exceed the ones in the authorised column, the train would be deemed fit to proceed and the slip handed to the driver.

A trip to Sandiacre was straightforward enough, but in theory T89 could be sent to any CE siding in the region. Although it was rare to venture much further than Toton, we did occasionally get sent to places as diverse as Burton, Loughborough, Stoke and Gloucester, which is why proper road learning was essential. In some cases, if the booked guard didn't sign the road, the secondman did and was able to conduct. Failing that, an unwitting, but 'competent' spare body would be plucked from the mess room on the outward journey.

Most of the time, the day's shunting would be completed within a couple of hours, and if there was no scheduled trip to Sandiacre or anywhere else, that was it for the day. The loco and crew couldn't just return to 4 Shed though. They had to justify their existence and would have to hide round at the sidings until at least six hours had elapsed. If it became apparent that there was going to be several hours of inactivity, the loco would be shut down and the teapot put to good use, or the crew would all suddenly turn into those toy dolls; the ones whose eyes automatically shut on any angle less than perpendicular. It isn't long, however, before train crew with time on their hands get up to some sort of mischief, and one day I played an ace.

I had been the guard all week and we had been busy, shunting here and tripping there, but in all that time the secondman had never lifted a finger to assist me. That he was a relief driver had a lot to do with it. A relief driver was just a trainman who had successfully completed the driving course and could undertake the odd driving turn, although usually nothing more than a Sprinter to Matlock, Nottingham or Crewe. In between these occasional driving turns, they still had to undertake normal trainman duties, but now they had taken another step towards becoming a registered driver, many refused to sign anywhere that involved getting their hands dirty. That being the case, they were either consistently booked as secondman or spare, which would leave them conveniently available for any possible driving turns. As a driving turn involved a higher rate of pay, many relief drivers could be found skulking in the mess room with the faint glimmer of pound signs in their eyes. Our secondman was no exception and was sat in the shunters' cabin with his feet up. The driver and I were still on the loco when the shunter climbed aboard and remarked on his laziness and how something should be done to get back at him. Cab phones hadn't been long introduced and were still very much in their infancy, but our loco had been fitted with one and I think the shunter and I noticed it at the same moment. It was obvious from our devious grins that we had both arrived at the same conclusion; it was time for a call. He gave me the number of his cabin, which I duly phoned. It was possible the secondman would ignore it, but surprisingly he answered, and I had to quickly effect the gruff, matter-of-fact voice of our senior TCS. Trying desperately not to laugh, I told him that he was needed for a driving turn and to report back to the shed straight away. My voice had been so unrealistic, that never for a second did I believe he'd fallen for it, so I put the phone down and tried to think of something else instead. I had, however, underestimated a relief drivers' avaricious nature, because suddenly the cabin door flew open and the secondman emerged, hurriedly pulling on his coat and signalling to us to pick him up. Rubbing our hands with gleeful delight, we pretended not to understand his wild gesticulations, so bag in hand he began running towards us.

"Look at this, it's the quickest he's moved all week," laughed the shunter.

Just as he was about to reach the loco, the driver put it in reverse and crept back slowly, making him run that little bit further. Eventually he caught up with us and I leaned out of the window.

"What's up, have you had a phone call?" I enquired innocently.

"Yes, I've got to get back to the shed immediately," he gasped between breaths.

"Was it the TCS?" I asked.

"Yes, come on, let's go!"

"No it wasn't...it was me."

I watched as the realization gradually sunk in, then he grabbed a handful of ballast and began throwing it at the cab. The driver and shunter were beside themselves, mainly because the secondman would have climbed up and throttled me if he hadn't been so out of breath. When we were next paired together, he got me back by re-arranging all the pages in my Rule Book and Working Manual, stripping the battery and bulb from my hand lamp and secreting the entire contents of my bag all around the sidings. I didn't mind too much, as I'd already taken the liberty of hiding a metal fishplate in his bag. These weighed about 4kgs and I believe he carried it around for two weeks before realizing...happy days!

Most of the fresh ballast for the weekend engineering trains was brought into Chadd' by the 91 Trip. Signing on at 07:30, another full train crew would depart 4 Shed in a pair of Class 20s (latterly a Class 31) and practically follow the Chadd' Shunt loco round to the sidings. Whilst the T89 loco and crew waited at the shunters' cabin, the guard from T91 would couple up and prepare his train of empties for their journey to Mountsorrel. This was the Redland Aggregates siding situated between Loughborough and Sileby, although the quarry itself was nearer Barrow-upon-Soar and the ballast was conveyed to the siding. On arrival at Sileby Junction, the train was required to propel into Mountsorrel, which I always considered to be an exceptionally dangerous move. For a start, we had to propel across both fast lines, which I found a little unnerving, particularly since HSTs rocketed up and down at about 100mph. I could only imagine the devastation if the signalman ever forgot we were there. The other worrying factor was that we were also propelling into Mountsorrel virtually blind. There were often two trains already in the siding and as our train snaked across the junction, it always looked as though we were on a collision course with them. The signalman wouldn't let us set back until the shunter at Mountsorrel had set an empty road and confirmed it of course but propelling into that siding always seemed like an act of pure blind faith to me. Because of the angle and length of the train, there was no possible way to see where you were heading until it was too late. Unfortunately, it took the death of yet another yard operative before other people realized this danger and operating procedures were changed.

Before the fatality, the loco would be run round in the siding and the wagons dragged through the loader. The guard would then complete his brake test and driver's slip and the train would be to return to Chaddesden. After the fatality, the train had to continue past Mountsorrel and run round at Humberstone Road sidings, just before Leicester station. On its return, it could then simply proceed straight into Mountsorrel, which was undoubtedly a lot safer.

20119 & 20066 awaiting their next turn of duty on the Machine Line, May 1992. This area was fully redeveloped into the modern Etches Park 'train care' depot fifteen years later. *Richard King.*

5. WEEKEND BALLAST

The CE department either sub-contracted or undertook most of infrastructure maintenance themselves, which could involve anything from a simple broken rail to large-scale engineering works. To minimise disruption to passenger services, large-scale work was generally carried out at weekends, commencing Saturday night and continuing into Sunday. At a pre-arranged hour, the signalman would grant the engineers possession of a section of running line. Most of these possessions would be granted after the last passenger service of the night or when trains could be successfully diverted. This possession would last for a set amount of time, within which the necessary work had to be completed. Once a possession had been granted, detonators, lookouts and illuminated marker boards would protect its entry and exit. Worksites could then be established within these boundaries, under the control of an engineering supervisor. Provided the signalman maintained his safety measures, there should be no unexpected visitors. Only the scheduled engineers' ballast trains would be allowed to proceed towards a possession, where they would wait at the marker boards for permission to enter.

A typical weekend engineering operation was re-ballasting, which involved sections of track being lifted and the old track bed removed. Fresh ballast would then be replaced and the track re-laid. Depending on which stage the work was at, trains would either arrive empty to be loaded with spoil or with fresh ballast for re-laying, or a combination of the two. At the worksite, most of the necessary plant, personnel and equipment would already be in place, which was an impressive logistical operation it itself, so all the train crew had to do was turn up with the wagons and work to instructions. Although re-ballasting constituted a large proportion of weekend work, other engineering jobs could include such things as cable laying, bridge inspections, cess clearance and tunnel repairs, and the trains would also bring some of the equipment to facilitate the task in hand. In each case, a full train crew was always required. Each weekend, there could be as many as eight different engineering jobs originating from Derby, so crews could find themselves scattered anywhere around the region. Leicester, Toton and some of the other remaining local depots also played their part in the work, whether providing trains and crews for their own allocated work, or relief crews for others. Up to 1992, the common form of traction for an engineering train was a pair of Class 20s, but as these were gradually withdrawn, a pair of Class 31s, or the odd Class 47 filled the void.

An engineers' ballast train had to be constantly manned throughout a weekend possession, so the train crew would normally be rotated over three shifts. For example, a crew signing on at 19:00 on Saturday would collect a train from Chadd' and take it to a particular worksite. The second crew, signing on around 02:00 on Sunday, would then be taken to the worksite by staff minibus or taxi to relieve the first. A final crew (if required) signing on around 08:00, also arriving at the worksite by motor transport, would relieve the second crew and eventually return the train to Chadd'. If you were scheduled to work, your booked time in the link usually determined which shift you ended up on. If you happened to be booked a Saturday rest day, you could opt to work that, as well as Sundays, for which a higher rate of pay was offered. In that case, the shift you ended up on was then governed by your next time on duty, as required periods of rest had to be observed.

To be honest, weekend engineering trains were largely undemanding for the train crew. Once in position at the worksite, the train was often not required to move again for the remainder of the shift, so the hardest part was probably signing on duty at such an anti-social hour in the first place and then coming to terms with the sheer boredom that followed. The driver and secondman would reside in the front cab, whilst the guard usually remained in the back cab, regrouping occasionally for a cuppa. In theory, front and rear end turns were distributed evenly throughout the trainman link, irrespective of whether you were a Trainman (D) or (G). In practice however, this was rarely the case. During my first year at Derby, I was often booked as secondman, but as my road knowledge and experience increased, and because I was consistently punctual, particularly during the small hours, I eventually reached a point where I was rarely considered for a front end ballast turn anymore. The relief drivers and other assorted shirkers thought they were getting one over on me, but this scenario suited me just fine. Once the initial guard duties had been completed, I preferred to be on my own in the back cab. That way, I was guaranteed not to have to endure any potentially frustrating company, except my own of course. Neither did I have to invent or engage in any pointless small talk, because even with a decent driver, the conversation topics eventually dried up. In short, I had the back cab all to myself and could set my stall out accordingly. I had peace in which to sit out the mind-numbing hours until the relief arrived.

Start times for a Saturday night ballast crew could range between 18:00 and 21:00, and after signing on, people would gather in the mess room and spend about fifteen minutes comparing their respective jobs, obtaining an adequate supply of water for the night and perhaps, more importantly, speculating on the alleged arrival time of their relief...then complaining to anyone who would listen. Although the mood was light-hearted, there was always a tiny bit of uncertainty as you departed, to who knew where for who knew how long? Not many people left the mess room without giving the shed men an envious glance either.

Saturday night ballast jobs all began the same way: light loco to Chadd' to collect the train. The guard would couple on and carry out the necessary checks before departure. As there were no lights in the sidings, this involved stumbling around the length of the train in relative darkness, depending on the season. In most cases, a Total Operations Processing System (TOPS) computer printed train list was available which incorporated a driver's slip at the bottom, so all the guard had to do was check the details and sign it before handing it to the driver. The signalman would be informed, and the train would then depart to its respective worksite, which could be just a few miles away or the other side of Northamptonshire. After departing Chadd', trains with a northbound destination had to be run round in the station yard first. Some trains were so long that the signalman had to talk them past DY449 (the starting signal on the Up Goods in the station). In this case, the guard would get on the phone and relay the signalman's instructions to the driver by hand signal. Once the last wagon had cleared the north end points, the signalman would inform the guard, who in turn would stop the train. He would then uncouple the loco and remain with the train, carrying out another brake test once the secondman had re-coupled at the other end.

Having been an outdoor worker of some description for most of my working life, I was never envious of the platelayers at the worksite. It was hard enough turning up at these unsocial hours in the first place, never mind labouring through them, in all weathers, to meet a strict deadline. I'm sure many of them saw us sitting in our cab, sheltered from the rain and cold and wished they could exchange places with us. However, like most things in life, our reality was often quite different. Sitting on a ballast job was essentially the same as sitting spare, except there were no comings or goings as there were in the mess room, and no potential for a change of scenery. A guard residing in the back cab could often go eight hours without seeing or talking to anyone. Try to imagine how that would feel next time you are in your own place of work. After a while, I began putting some of this dead time to use and completed a correspondence course in vehicle mechanics, started learning a second language and even began writing notes for a future book. Of course, the irregular hours played havoc with your body clock and digestive system and from the idling locomotive(s), came the constant sweet, sickly smell of diesel fumes, which contributed further to this unhappy human condition. In effect, the whole experience was largely uncomfortable, unfulfilling and above all, mentally and physically debilitating, which in a perverse sort of way, was worse than any physical labour. Even sleep offered little release, and although enginemen have the reputation of being able to sleep anywhere, I never could, unless it was in an actual bed.

As much as I liked Class 20s, they were a damn uncomfortable loco to reside in for any length of time. The chairs were basic and most had no armrests. The secondman or guard could rest his feet on the handbrake wheel in front of him, but with no other leg support, this position quickly became uncomfortable. Similarly, he could swivel his chair round and rest his legs on the driving desk behind, but this was a rather cramped position. I eventually resorted to placing my smock on the floor and stretching out fully behind the chairs, which was ideal for me. I can't say it was ideal for a certain guard who relieved me once though, because as he pushed open the door where my feet were and began climbing up into the cab, I rose in the gloom like Dracula from his coffin. He had the shock of his life as our faces met just above floor level, so much so, that he fell off the steps in shock.

Class 47s were slightly more comfortable but the high-pitched scream of the air compressor kicking in every twenty minutes had the potential to drive you insane after a while...which might explain a few things.

As the hours ticked slowly by, only three things remained foremost in the minds of a crew waiting for relief; what time do the relief sign on, how long will it take them to get here, and will they be able to find the worksite when they do? On paper, each shift roughly equated to eight hours on duty, but ten and twelve hours were commonplace. This owed, in part, to the relief timings rarely considering the travelling time to and from a worksite. A crew stuck near Luton would obviously have a longer wait for relief, and subsequent journey back to 4 Shed than a crew who had remained within a twenty-mile radius of Derby. The timings also didn't allow for unreliable trainmen not turning up for duty in the small hours, delays with the motor transport and the time it could take a relief crew to find an obscure worksite in the middle of nowhere.

Having a worksite on a main line and arriving by rail was simple. Trying to reach it by road in the middle of the night was something entirely different. For some of the more nondescript trackside locations, the taxi or minibus carrying the relief crew could spend a while travelling up and down dark country lanes, its occupants desperately scanning the surrounding area for any evidence of railway activity. As the vehicle may have changed direction several times during the search, eventual arrival at the site could be disorientating for the crew. In the absence of any distinguishing landmarks or lineside features, it could often be difficult to ascertain which direction the train was facing, and more importantly, if the job had been run round yet. If it hadn't, there was a distinct possibility that it would have to be done during your shift. Also, the train you were relieving could be in a cutting, on a viaduct, up an embankment, or on rare occasions, in a tunnel. At the very least, the relieving crew would usually have to climb over a fence or traverse a field to reach the track. The likes of Big Bill trying to squeeze himself and his provisions through a barbed wire fence at 03:00 on a Sunday morning were always a highlight.

Just because a crew had been relieved and were happily ensconced in the minibus awaiting the journey home, it didn't necessarily mean all their problems were over. Some of the transport drivers had been on for hours and the drink-driving rule wasn't always strictly adhered to by some of them. Consequently, there were many instances where transport drivers have nodded off whilst returning crews home. Once when we were on the M1 travelling back to 4 Shed from a job, our driver veered from the fast lane right across to the hard shoulder and back again. A reasonably clear indication that he had fallen asleep at the wheel, awoken at the last second then drastically over compensated for his mistake. Fortunately, the traffic had been light at that time in the morning, but one Derby crew wasn't so lucky when their minibus overturned under similar circumstances. Although some of their injuries were severe, they were all fortunately able to return to work in due course.

I think the most sought-after ballast job on a Saturday night was probably the 17:45 Bedford, which tended to crop up every so often. This was a nice straightforward run from Chadd' to Bedford, where the crew would be relieved in the station before returning home on the next passenger service. Its main attraction was the achievable and generally guaranteed finish time, but this depended entirely on the mood of the signalman at West Hampstead PSB, and the Bedford TCS.

There were few surprises to be had during the steady run to Bedford, although after Kettering, the train could sometimes be routed onto the slow line at Harrowden Junction (or Weetabix Junction as it was sometimes called, since the factory was situated right next to the track), so if the guard hadn't been paying attention from the back cab, he would suddenly find his train temporarily diverging from the main lines after Wellingborough, to pass through Sharnbrook (or Wymington) Tunnel. Once over Sharnbrook Summit, the tracks would converge at Sharnbrook Junction again, but the train would continue along the Up Slow, where it would finally be held at Bedford North. There the train would stand until the Bedford crew signed on, at which point, the signalman would finally allow it into the station for relief.

The waiting time at Bedford North could range between one and two hours and was dependent on the relief crew signing on at the correct hour and the time of the possession they were eventually working the train forward to. Although the Derby crew were booked to return home on a specific passenger train, this didn't stop them from trying to get into Bedford straight away, to try to catch an earlier service. Some people would be on the signal phone every fifteen minutes, asking if the train could be allowed into the station, whereupon it could be secured in one of the platforms and everyone could disappear on the next available train home. Although it probably only meant gaining two hours or so, it was the difference between finishing still within the boundaries of Saturday night, or in the early hours of Sunday morning. It was often amusing to listen to the tone of those requests from crew members who had a vested interest in finishing early, usually to catch last orders. They always began amiably enough then degenerated into frustration, and finally threats of leaving the train as more and more time passed by. Nevertheless, it *was* frustrating to be sat less than half a mile from your destination and watch each northbound HST pass by on its way back to Derby. To add insult to injury, it was usually a Derby man at the controls, so he'd whistle up and make a drinking motion with his hand as he rocketed past. Once the train had been allowed to proceed into the station for relief, the previous frustrations were quickly forgotten and the crew able to relax on the homeward journey. Although the job often only equated to a seven-hour shift (which was exceptionally rare for a weekend ballast job), the booked passenger train stopped at most of the major stations along the route and called at Nottingham before finally pulling into Derby around 00:30, which is why most of the crews tried to get an earlier, faster and more direct service.

There were a couple of occasions when the job wasn't always so clean cut because of staff availability at Bedford. Once, owing to a clerical error, we arrived at Bedford to find no relief booked on, so we had to work the train forward to Cricklewood and stable it in the recess sidings. Ordinarily, this would have been fine, provided motor transport had been laid on for us between Cricklewood and St. Pancras (roughly six miles), but as no one seemed to have any record of us after Bedford, we were left completely to our own devices. We didn't exist on paper therefore we didn't exist at all. In the end, we had to walk to Cricklewood station, catch the next local service to Luton, board another local service from there back to Kings Cross Thameslink, before finally walking the short distance to St. Pancras. By this time, we were seriously in danger of missing the last train home, but, amazingly, the station staff had been informed of our predicament and had held the train for us, some of them even cheered as we ran down the platform. Another time, a Bedford guard didn't turn up for duty and I was asked to remain with the train. I was working my rest day on that occasion, which meant I would be on double time after midnight, but the thought of spending another thirteen hours (best case scenario), on top of the three I'd already worked, was just too much to bear, so I declined. Besides, I'd already consumed all my provisions on the journey which, coincidently, broke the first rule of weekend ballast working: always save something for the twelfth hour.

Regardless of the myriad health and safety legislation that some people presume will automatically shield them from every mortal danger, accidents do happen, and the very nature of railway work constantly exposed its personnel to life threatening situations, whether they were always consciously aware of it or not. Sometimes though, these life-threatening situations were entirely of our own making, with of course, a little bit of fate thrown in.

One Saturday night, I pulled out of Chadd' with perhaps the longest train I'd ever worked. It must have been about half a mile in length, and with a pair of Class 31s on the front, it looked like a real monster. Just preparing it in the sidings meant I'd already walked a fair distance. The worksite was scheduled to be between Wichnor Junction and Tamworth station, and we were required to wait in Elford Loop until the last passenger service had passed, at which point the possession would be granted. After safely clearing the main line, we waited in the loop as instructed. Presently, the engineering supervisor appeared to discuss forthcoming train movements. Having already cleared it with the signalman, he asked if our train could set back towards the trap points at the entrance of the loop. (Should a train depart from a loop or sidings without permission, trap points derail the offending train clear of any running lines.) It seemed a pointless move to me, and considering the length of our train, one that I wasn't particularly keen to undertake. However, apart from a sense of foreboding, I didn't have any definite objections as to why it couldn't be done, so after consulting with my driver, I walked back to check the available distance. Elford Loop is just under a mile long (remember what I said about proper road learning), so I had roughly half a mile to play with. It was dark by this time, and I knew the length of our train would cause some difficulties, but the driver was watching for my signal, so using my hand lamp, I waved a green light across my body, which was the signal to set back slowly, at caution. Immediately after I'd given it, my lamp went dead. The battery was completely flat and there was now no way of signalling the driver to stop. Unusually for a ballast crew, we were all still in our early twenties; the secondman was a renowned layabout, and the driver, without sounding nasty, wasn't overly bright, or adequately experienced with this kind of work. I don't know what he was thinking, but to my horror, he opened up fully and the train began setting back at an alarming rate. I waved my arms about like some demented windmill, but to no avail. I knew from experience that the secondman wouldn't even be looking anyway. Any normal person shunting at night, particularly under these circumstances, would have maintained a continuous signal with their hand lamp, primarily to reassure the driver that he was still proceeding as required. I would have done this had I been able, but in the absence of any further signals, the driver should have stopped immediately. This evidently wasn't happening.

There was only one way to stop the train now and that was pull the vacuum pipe off the last wagon, but as they were passing me at roughly 10mph, I would have to run like a maniac to catch up with the last one. I would have beaten any Olympic sprinter that night, as I raced down the ballast towards the end of the train. With a supreme effort, resulting largely from a mixture of adrenalin and pure terror, I climbed into the last wagon and reached over the side to pull the pipe off, but it was well out of my grasp. The trap points were looming dangerously close now, but the sheer exertion had left me completely breathless and I was at a loss what to do next. It's true I could have let the wagons run through the trap points, into the buffer stops and down the embankment, but I couldn't be sure that on hitting the buffer stops, they wouldn't ride over each other, rear up in the air and foul the main line. The last express was imminent and there was absolutely no way of stopping it. Also, it suddenly dawned on me that I was riding in the last wagon, so even if they did all tumble down the bank and onto what looked like a concrete hard standing twenty feet below, I would be a certain fatality. Kicking the pipe off was now the only viable option.

To achieve this miracle, I had to climb over the side of the wagon and hang onto the left-hand buffer sleeve, whereupon I could dangle my legs either side of the rail until my heels were dragging in the ballast. From this position, I was able to kick at the pipe with my right foot, all too aware of the burnished wagon wheel rapidly revolving between my legs, which would immediately slice me in half if I lost my grip. It took a few attempts, but my foot finally hit the pipe and it flew of its dummy connector. There was a noisy inrush of air as the vacuum was destroyed, and with much relief, I half jumped, half fell clear as the brakes began to apply. I knew I'd taken a terrible risk, but I was a lot younger then, and youth coupled with agility had triumphed in the end. The severe and unexpected brake application must have virtually put the driver and secondman through the cab windscreen, but it was nothing less than they deserved. I was unable to worry about it, because at that moment, I was practically unconscious on the track, desperately trying to suck some air into my tortured lungs. The train came to a stand about six wagon lengths away from the trap points, seconds before the last express hurtled past on its way to Birmingham. The driver and secondman eventually came running up the track to try to ascertain what had happened, and if I hadn't been so spent, I would have knocked their silly heads together. Instead, I contented myself that at least one of them had a bloody nose from where it had obviously connected with the windscreen. My train positioning turned out to be perfect for the engineering supervisor, who incidentally, remained completely oblivious to the terrible disaster I'd unwittingly set in motion then subsequently managed to avert. Unlike some 'senior condom' that had just raised his ticket sales by five percent, no Silver Swift* (The InterCity Achievement Award) was ever pinned on my chest. The incident was never reported, although I did have a few quiet words with my supposed crew members, when I eventually got my breath back.

CE-liveried 31126 heads a ballast train at Trent South Junction, November 1991. *Richard King.*

*In typical railway style, the powers-that-be decided that the InterCity logo was a swallow rather than a swift, when surely the latter would have been (generally) more appropriate.

6. CLIFFE HILL 1990

The Leicester & Burton Line (Part 1)

The Cliffe Hill job was the archetypal ballast working, and for most new trainmen at Derby, the first 'main line' route that they learnt. All those weeks of rules and regulations suddenly began to make some sense and would undoubtedly be employed along this interesting, varied and challenging route. It was classic railway work and an excellent job to learn on because it could throw anything and everything at you, and often did, given enough time.

It was also an opportunity to work with and get to know some of the old-hand drivers who were regulars on the run. Characters like Driver Welsh for instance, who was a World War Two naval veteran and close to retirement. He reminded me of an aged version of Popeye, in both manner and speech, and was famous for referring to everyone as "brothel bred scum." He was also famous, or rather infamous, for his driver's bag, the sole contents of which consisted of his lunch for the day, two very graphic adult magazines and a large black marital aid. Initially, in my naivety, I thought he was a snake enthusiast of some sort because almost everyone used to enquire about his black mamba. I don't know what the traction inspectors made of it, but it was an excellent prop for a bit of tomfoolery. On entering the mess room, he would usually label everyone as "brothel bred scum" before proceeding to fill his large teapot. Next, he would sing a crude song or recite a dirty limerick whilst completing his timesheet, regardless that he hadn't yet done any work. It was then either a quick showing of the bag interior to a hushed and awestruck group or a chance to use his other favourite catchphrase on some unsuspecting individual. "Do you want to see my war wound?" he'd ask, before parting his hair slightly to reveal a scar. "Someone smashed a bottle on my head in a brothel in Algeria in 1942."

The purpose of the job was to fetch railway ballast for the CE department, for use in their track maintenance programmes on the Eastern Region, and there were two daily runs to Cliffe Hill. The first originated from Doncaster Wood Yard and the second from Healey Mills. Our signing on times were 06:01 and 11:28 respectively and we relieved the Eastern Region drivers, usually at signal DY449. Often it would be a Class 47 taking the strain, but occasionally, a Class 37 would make an appearance. The train itself was vacuum braked, usually with a mixture of ZFV, ZEV, ZJV and YGH ballast wagons. These code letters were the TOPS computer classifications, but most of the wagons in the CE fleet still retained their old telegraphic code names, which were all associated with the sea in some way. Therefore, to us, these wagons were better known as Dogfish, Catfish, Mermaid and Sealion. Sometimes a ZUV (Shark) plough brakevan would be included in the formation as well. Once relieved, the Eastern Region driver would return home on the next passenger train, whilst the trainman was informing the signalman that 7M74 was ready to depart.

Once the road had been given, a couple of notches on the power handle would set the train heading west out of Derby and through its environs of Peartree and Sunnyhill towards Stenson Junction. Willington Power Station would be passed on the left, then over North Stafford Junction before reaching Clay Mills Level Crossing. This was a place you would smell first before seeing, as there was a sewage farm situated right next to the crossing. There were also hot axle box detectors there, so if there was a problem with the train, now was the time to find out. If there happened to be an express following behind, the train could be switched onto the Down Goods at this point as well. Rounding the corner after Clay Mills, the digital clock on the Bass brewery tower could be observed, its display alternating between the current time and temperature. If you were with one old-hand driver, he would always remark on the time saying, "We're a bit later/earlier than yesterday mate" so of course, your standard reply would always be "It's a bit colder/warmer today though." It was just one of those little rituals that had to be observed. The train would now be well and truly on the approach to Burton-upon-Trent, a place with its own distinctive smell, slightly more pleasant than the last one, one of beer brewing. After passing Wetmore Sidings, the train would proceed steadily through Platform 2, if it were still on the main line, or adjacent to it, if on the Down Goods. Either way, the route indicator signal would be lit, and the train would be switched onto the Leicester & Burton Line at Leicester Junction, just after the end of the platform.

As the train snaked its way round towards Birmingham Curve Junction, the wagon wheels would always squeal terribly, no doubt in protest about being dragged around such a tight curve. I often expected a resident from nearby Cambridge or Oxford Street to complain, but living in the shadow of Drakelow Power Station, I suppose they were more than used to it. Once over the River Trent, the train would then pass through the well-used Drakelow West and East Junctions. Drakelow B and C stations consumed a lot of coal and there always seemed to be a train arriving, unloading or departing. To feed Drakelow's large appetite, the first half of the Leicester & Burton Line was dominated solely by coal extraction. The next point was Swadlincote Junction, which was a misnomer, as there was no junction there at the time. There used to a spur from the Up Goods to Cadley Hill Colliery, which had been taken out. This was replaced again in 1992, to serve Nadins opencast disposal point. After Swadlincote, the one and only tunnel on the route would be encountered. At 623 yards, Gresley Tunnel wasn't particularly long, but a bit of an oddity in that it (eventually) ended up with two speed limits. Going through on the Up Goods, the limit was 45mph, but coming the other way on the Down Goods, it was only 10mph. No one ever seemed to have a plausible explanation for this, although I think it is safe to assume that mining subsidence had a lot to do with it. One theory is that the Down Goods had been severely twisted because of this subsidence, and as wagons tend to sway at speed, the limit was considerably lowered to prevent them from making contact with the tunnel wall. Once this theory had been digested, I always found it a little unnerving to return with a loaded train through the tunnel. I used to wince involuntarily each time, expecting a wagon to connect with the brickwork and throw us off the track at any moment.

Visual evidence of the mining subsidence became apparent after Gresley Tunnel, as both tracks appeared alarmingly sunken and twisted, earning this spot the nickname of 'The Big Dipper'. Signalling control now passed from Derby PSB to Moira West Signal Box, and just after the train rattled through Moira West Junction, the box would be passed on the right. Opposite Moira box was Rawdon Colliery and its associated sidings. Trains were still operating out of there but during my tenure on the Cliffe Hill the colliery was eventually dismantled. Passing the last few active re-workings of Swains Park opencast, the track would then change to single line at Lounge Junction. Lounge Disposal Point would be on the left and signal control would change again to Mantle Lane Signal Box. Once through Swannington Crossing, the train would enter the aptly named Coalville, with the depot on the right and Mantle Lane box opposite. This was where the trainman would normally 'bail out' to stop the driver once the end of the train had cleared the shunt signal. The signalman would then set the road and the trainman would call the driver back into the reception sidings for a wagon examination.

Wagon examiners used cards to indicate any faults they found and would attach them to the offending vehicles accordingly. Predominantly green in colour, these cards allowed further travel but with certain restrictions imposed. For example, some were marked with a reduced speed, others stated that the wagon was not to be loaded, and so forth. For a serious fault however, a red card would be produced, which simply stated: Not To Go. This would be an unwelcome development, as the train crew would have to shunt the train and remove the crippled wagon. An old chap, who had been given the nickname of 'Red Card Jack' by some of the Derby drivers, often conducted the wagon examination. I'm not sure how he earned his nickname because out of all the trains I worked through Coalville, I only ever had to knock out one crippled wagon. Driver Welsh was less than convinced though and would always remark, "Here comes stop 'em Jack...brothel bred scum!" before breaking into a song about someone called Dirty Sally...

Whilst the train was undergoing its examination, the crew could either go on a tea foraging mission to Coalville mess room or perhaps partake of some footplate cuisine. One of the regular old-hand drivers used to cook himself a full English breakfast on the loco hotplate each morning. Instead of traction manuals, rule books and weekly notices, his driver's bag contained eggs, bacon, sausages and the all-important frying pan. I believe Driver Welsh also ran his video empire from Coalville mess room, so he would often nip across to tantalize the lads with the latest releases or to collect any returns, although I doubt any of the titles would have appeared on a family viewing list. Once the wagon examination had been completed,

Jack would give the thumbs-up and shout "OK!" but Driver Welsh would pretend to be engrossed in one of his artistic magazines, so Jack would walk round to his side of the cab and shout again, but to no avail. In the end he would have to climb up into the cab, "What's up driver, are you deaf?" he would ask, allowing Driver Welsh to launch into another one of his favourite catchphrases.

"Deaf? You'd be deaf too, if you were on a battleship when a bomb came down the funnel and knocked all the crockery of the shelves."

Once it was established that we were clear to proceed, the signalman would set the road and the train would draw out onto double track again, through Coalville Station Crossing with its distinctive, but now disused signal box, and on towards Coalville Junction. Coalfields Farm would be passed on the right, the last coal loading facility of the route at the time. The signalling responsibility would change again to Bardon Hill and the train would begin its climb towards the signal box and level crossing, passing Bardon Hill sidings on the left. Finally, Cliffe Hill would be in sight and the train would draw up to No2 ground frame, situated near the B585 over bridge. The trainman would uncouple the loco, get the release for the ground frame from Bardon Hill box and set the road for the loco to run round. Often, the driver wouldn't bother changing ends, so the trainman would jump into the now leading cab, as the loco propelled down to No1 ground frame. This frame was electronic and at the push of a button, the trainman would set the road onto the wagons, call the driver back and re-couple the loco. During my first few runs as a novice trainman, I was always very wary about leaving the wagons on such a steep gradient whilst we ran round. According to the Rule Book, you were supposed to apply several wagon handbrakes, but as I was reliably informed, and as I eventually found out myself through experience, the chances of vacuum braked wagons rolling away were extremely remote. Nevertheless, I often imagined the nightmare scenario of runaway wagons at Cliffe Hill and was always secretly relieved when the loco was re-coupled to the train. The whole train would then draw out past No1 frame and the trainman would push the button to set the road into Cliffe Hill (Tarmac) siding, before finally calling the driver back again. Once the train had set back into the siding, a series of lights controlled its movements during loading. The trainman would return control of the ground frame to the signalman, complete the necessary brake test and prepare a driver's slip, ready for the return journey. If he was a conscientious chap, he might also take the opportunity to examine each wagon after loading, just to ascertain there was no loose ballast anywhere. Once up to speed on the main line, these individual stones could become high velocity projectiles, which posed an obvious danger to passing trains. There had been a few incidents of HSTs getting their carriage windows smashed whilst hurtling past ballast trains, so it eventually became a requirement to remove any ballast overspill.

Once loading had been completed, usually after two or three hours, the trainman would obtain permission to set the road onto the Down Goods, and the now designated (6 or 7) E85 would be ready to depart. After a brief stop at Coalville to collect the TOPS list, and another wagon examination, it would be a steady run back to Birmingham Curve Junction. The train would often be held there to await a path back onto the Derby-Birmingham Line. There was a recreation ground situated close to the track and whilst we were waiting one day, I noticed a lad with a dog standing on top of the slide. The dog was on a lead and watching us, but the lad was totally oblivious and was trying to encourage his pet down the slide. Eventually, the signalman cleared the signal and the driver gave a toot on the horn. Unfortunately, this startled the dog, which dragged its hapless owner face first down the slide. They both ended up in a heap at the bottom, but the lad managed to pick himself and give us several vigorous two-fingered salutes before we disappeared. I didn't stop laughing until Clay Mills.

The only other delay might occur just before Derby. If the train happened to be running early, it would be routed into the loop at Sunnyhill whilst the relieving Eastern Region driver was located. Otherwise, it was straight into Platform 1 for relief and then back to 4 Shed to sign off duty. At 4 Shed, the TCS and roster clerk were seated behind a window and train crew would deposit their timesheets into a hatch underneath. On several occasions, Driver Welsh also deposited the fabled marital aid, much to the shock and annoyance of the roster clerk.

In general, the job was well structured and seemed to operate efficiently. However, its days were numbered. By the end of 1990, Cliffe Hill was rendered obsolete and a new working devised into Stud Farm. Although Stud Farm was situated literally at the back of Cliffe Hill, it could only be accessed from the Leicester direction, so a group of us were sent to learn the second half of the line. Cliffe Hill wasn't the only place to be rendered obsolete in 1990; Coalville depot was also closed in October of that year. Its proud men were scattered to the four winds, although at least one of their number fetched up on our shores and was able to take a handful of Derby drivers and trainmen road learning. The marital aid was also retired, along with Driver Welsh.

7. STUD FARM 1991

The Leicester & Burton Line (Part 2)

No2 ground frame at Cliffe Hill marked the edge of the known world for me. I didn't sign any further and everything after that was an undiscovered country. After months of running round and returning home from this point, it seemed strange to contemplate venturing any further. In this seemingly lonely, desolate place, who would want to go further? But what lay beyond Cliffe Hill? We were the Derby pioneers. During February 1991, a small group of drivers and trainmen were given two days' road learning Stud Farm. This involved taking a spare loco off the shed and travelling the length of the Leicester & Burton Line (roughly 30 miles), concentrating primarily on the Leicester end and the movements in Stud Farm itself. On the first day we rattled up and down the line in a pair of Class 20s (20058 & 20087), then on the second day it was the turn of 47973, all regular Derby locos.

After Cliffe Hill No2 frame, the next point was Bagworth Junction, which was the access into Stud Farm, but only from the Leicester direction, unless of course you were light loco, in which case you could go behind the shunt signal, change ends and drive in. At 565 feet, Bagworth Summit was the highest point on the line, and where signalling control changed from Bardon Hill to Leicester PSB. After that it was a rapid single line descent down to Desford Crossing, past the golf course and through another level crossing at Kirby Muxloe, before heading into the more depressed area of Braunstone on the outskirts of Leicester. Once across Aylestone Viaduct, past Vic Berry's scrapyard and the small power station at Saffron Lane, it was merely a case of awaiting the signalman's pleasure to cross you over the main lines at Knighton Junction and into the passing loop. Once in the loop, it was either back to Derby via Burton or Leicester, the latter being the quickest. Waiting at Knighton (allegedly) had its compensations, as the cab was level with the bedroom windows of the nearby houses. According to legend, there was supposed to be a woman in the end house who always did aerobics in the nude. I never saw her and no one I worked with ever did, but it was always mentioned, and we always looked.

The basic structure of the Cliffe Hill job remained the same, only the timings and destination changed. The signing on times were now 06:09 and 09:54 and the first runs began in March. The Stud Farm facility was supposed to be a step forward, but I could never understand why it had been designed with single line access from one direction only, and why it could only accommodate one train at a time, but then again, I was just a lowly trainman. To compound those errors, the powers-that-be, in their wisdom, decided our two jobs would have to go via Burton, both on the outward *and* return journey. To put that into perspective, it meant plodding up to Cliffe Hill as normal, carrying on past Stud Farm and continuing all the way down to Knighton, where the loco would be run round, ready to drag the train all the way back up to Stud Farm. After loading, it would be back down to Knighton to run round, before traversing the Leicester & Burton Line in its entirety again, to finally end up at Derby for relief; a torturous 108-mile trip. Why we couldn't go via Leicester each way, I'll never know, although I seem to recall a familiar and often used phrase at the time; 'pathing problems'. Another problem was that there were at least two other jobs into Stud Farm besides ours, and as everything seemed to run hideously late most of the time, we often tended to clash. Arriving relatively trouble free at Stud Farm, albeit in a roundabout sort of way, didn't always guarantee immediate access. If there happened to be one of those jobs already loading, your train would have to set back into the refuge siding and wait its turn – a truly painful experience all round.

The movements once inside Stud Farm were straightforward; the train would proceed over the weighbridge on slow speed (half a mile an hour) and continue along the loading road. Once in clear, the loco would be run round and the wagons propelled back until the first one was positioned under the loader. It would then simply be a case of drawing forward to load each wagon, under the control of the bunker staff using a two-way radio. The resident 'tapper' would carry out a wagon examination, and once loading had been completed, there would be a further wait for the train list to be printed before proceeding slowly over the weighbridge once more and final departure in the Leicester direction. Waiting for the train list added insult to injury. Sometimes it would be 40 minutes or more before TOPS Control decided to send it through, but for some unknown reason, the train was not allowed to depart without it. Why a manual train list and a driver's slip were not considered enough for the return journey, I never understood.

I believe only four trainmen signed Stud Farm initially and I was one of them. I can't blame people for avoiding the job, it was a regular twelve-hour shift, and that was only if it ran to some sort of schedule. After the carefree innocence of Cliffe Hill, this job came as a bit of a shock and could be soul-destroying if you weren't prepared for it. The best strategy was to accept that it was going to be a long day, set your stall out and just think of the overtime. I regularly averaged a seventy-hour week, with a personal best of ninety-six hours in one week, although that was with a rest day and a Sunday included. (Maximum working time regulations had yet to be introduced.)

My other claim to fame was a fifteen-hour day, owing to our loco failing at Bagworth. The driver and I were on the 06:09 job, had loaded the train, run round at Knighton and were making good progress from Desford up to Bagworth. Once we hit the steep incline though, our weary Class 47 got slower and slower, eventually coming to a stand about half way up. No amount of coaxing could get it moving again, so I walked up to the signal phone at Bagworth and informed Bardon Hill of our predicament. The signalman told me that an assisting loco would arrive in the rear, from Leicester depot I assumed. That sounded promising, as there was always a good spread of Class 47s, 56s and 58s to choose from – plenty of motive power to push our train up the incline. On hearing this, the signalman laughed "Oh no, you can't have any of those locos, they're a different sector to you." Don't we all work for the same railway I wondered? "Besides, your assisting loco is coming from Wellingborough," he added. The available locos at Leicester were most likely coal, parcels or even construction livery, but because we were officially a departmental train, they couldn't be allowed to assist us, all because of a different colour scheme.

After informing my driver, I walked to the rear of our train, put down detonator protection and waited for the assisting loco. My all-enduring memory of the Leicester & Burton Line is that it always seemed cold. The spot where we were stuck was particularly windswept and I was freezing. It was beginning to get dark and there was still no sign of our assistance. I walked back to the loco to fetch my hand lamp and have a quick warm, before returning to my lonely vigil at the furthest detonator. After another hour of waiting, I walked all the way back up to Bagworth to contact the signalman again, only for him to tell me the loco had been delayed – as if I didn't know! Apart from occasional trips to the loco, I remained waiting at the furthest detonator. Eventually, far off in the darkness, I could hear a distant rumble. First it would seem close, then the sound would disappear altogether, and I began to think I was imagining things, until finally the sound of an approaching loco was unmistakable.

After four hours, our rescue finally came in the form of a single Class 31 – in BR blue livery – from Wellingborough. What a way to run a railway! After checking its approach with my hand lamp, I climbed aboard. The deathly silence I'd grown accustomed to was suddenly punctuated with the shocking noise of my detonators exploding under its wheels as we continued towards the rear of our train. After conferring with my driver and the signalman, we were ready for the big push and whistled up accordingly. The amp gauge in the Class 31 probably melted, but somehow this little loco managed to shove us up the bank and we were able to propel our wagons into the refuge siding at Stud Farm. I secured the wagons and coupled the two locos together for a brisk run down to Knighton and an eventual weary arrival on Leicester shed. My driver and I managed to catch the next passenger train to Derby, but we didn't get off the hook that easily. The next day, after we'd had our required twelve hours rest, it was light loco to collect our wagons and complete the job.

It was obvious, even to us at ground level that things couldn't continue the way they were. Train crews were beginning to abandon the job after eight hours, leaving the wagons in Knighton Old Sidings and returning to Derby light loco, and who could blame them? No matter how enthusiastic or dedicated you were, the timings were simply unworkable. By the end of July, the Stud Farm job was shelved as far as Derby men were concerned and a new working devised into Bardon Hill.

N1 and N2 occupied on night shed, October 1993. *Richard King*.

47344 loading at Stud Farm, June 1991. *Richard King*.

Headed by 56020, the 'Denby' is ready to depart from Kilburn, January 1992. *Author*.

8. BARDON HILL 1991-93

The Leicester & Burton Line (Part 3)

It must have been around 05:00 on a fresh January morning, as I squeezed between the loco and first wagon at Knighton, attempting to disconnect the icy vacuum pipe and coupling. I had on about five layers of clothing, but it didn't make any difference, the cold still cut straight through me and we hadn't even set off up to Bagworth yet. Cold? I don't think I'd ever been so cold in all my life. The 'old-hands' used to say that when you were on Bag'orth Summit, the next highest point as the crow flies was Siberia, and that's where the cold came from. Now being a veteran on the line, I was quite prepared to believe it.

To be honest, I didn't care much for the Bardon Hill job. Its only saving grace was that we were finally operating on the route as we should have done all along. The outward journey was now via Leicester, run round at Knighton, straight up the Leicester & Burton Line to Bardon Hill, where the trainman would use the ground frame and set the train back into the sidings. He would then uncouple the loco and Bardon's own shunting loco would collect the wagons and take them into the quarry to be loaded. After which, it was back to Derby via Burton – all very straightforward. The signing on times for the train crew were now 03:35 and 07:14 respectively. The 07:14 job was tolerable, but I always found 03:35 a punishing time to start work, especially in the depths of winter. It was also a notorious time for people not turning up, so if you happened to be 00:05 spare, there was a good chance you would be sent in their stead. That was not a pleasant prospect when you had been sat in the mess room over three hours and were hoping for an early finish.

The journey to Leicester at that time in the morning always seemed grey and uneventful and there was little conversation to be had. Even if you had a decent driver for company, no one felt like talking. Besides, there was nothing to comment on, the rest of the world was still asleep, and you really wished you could join them.

It always felt cold running round at Knighton, regardless of the time of year. Once uncoupled, I tended to wait with the train whilst the loco proceeded to Wigston Junction, returning on the main line to be put back into the loop. There were a variety of ways the signalman at Leicester PSB could do this and there seemed to be a different method every day. Even some of the very experienced drivers weren't sure of all the moves, so the trainman's knowledge became invaluable. It could be an odd experience advising a senior top-link driver how to run round at Knighton. Once the loco had been re-coupled, the trainman would walk to the rear of the train, fit a tail lamp to the last wagon and perform a brake test. Whilst walking the length of the train, you would sometimes encounter a wall of heat, which was most unnatural considering the ambient temperature. This phenomenon immediately indicated that the wagon nearest to you was suffering from dragging brakes. After ascertaining its handbrake was fully off, the next step was to pull the vacuum release string and kick the brake blocks to ensure they had been released properly.

Once accepted onto the Leicester & Burton Line, you were normally the first morning train to negotiate the single line through the rather dubious area of Braunstone, so it wasn't uncommon to come across the ubiquitous supermarket trolley placed strategically on the track, or even the odd washing machine, as was the case for one crew. On arrival at Bardon Hill Sidings, the trainman would alight near the ground frame whilst the train continued clear of the points. After ensuring all the necessary hand points were set for an empty road, he would then operate the frame and call the driver back into the sidings. It was important for the trainman to make a physical check of the hand points, as what often appeared to be an empty road, sometimes wasn't. Bardon Aggregates shared this siding with Prismo Bitumen and it wasn't uncommon to find wagons left foul. It was just one of those places where it was so easy to slip up, particularly during the early hours. Also, no matter where you stood, you could never see the end of the train as it set back into the sidings, so you were never quite sure what you were setting back onto, particularly as there was an internal vehicle crossing to consider as well.

My other dislike of the job was the interminable waiting around in the sidings. Once the shunter had coupled on and dragged the wagons away, there was nothing to do; there wasn't even any scenery to look at. At least at Cliffe Hill or Stud Farm, you were an active part of the loading process. You could see how many wagons had been loaded and how many were left, and more importantly, you could roughly gauge when you'd be heading home again, but there was none of this interaction at Bardon Hill. Two of Bardon's own men operated the shunt loco, but their brusque manner never really endeared them to me, especially during the bleak early hours. Once our loco had been uncoupled, the wagons were supposed to be their responsibility, but they always seemed reluctant to emerge from their loco for any great length of time. As our trains were all vacuum braked and their shunt loco was air only, they left it to the trainman to pull the vacuum release strings on every wagon, so they could just couple on and drag them away. If the train wasn't fully prepared when they decided to collect it, I often used to find that it had been interfered with on its return; perhaps a wagon handbrake applied somewhere, several instanter couplings changed to the long position or the tail light missing – all rather petty and unnecessary. As our trains became longer, the internal vehicle crossing became fouled also. Local instructions dictated that BR staff were not permitted to split the train in the sidings, so the lorry drivers would complain to the signalman, who would phone the local traffic manager, who would tell us to split the train, whom we in turn would inform that the wagons were not our responsibility in the sidings – and around it would go. As I said, all very unnecessary, simply because the wagons couldn't be dragged clear immediately on our arrival.

As basic communication, common sense and courtesy often seemed in short supply, it was always a relief to depart Bardon Hill and head for home. The last remaining obstacle was still Sunnyhill loop though, and the waiting time for both jobs seemed to have increased drastically. On average, it could be an hour or more before the signalman at Derby PSB allowed you into the station for relief. Sometimes you would sit there so long that you would begin to hallucinate. More than once, a driver has suddenly awoken from a half doze, flicked the controller from 'engine only' to 'forward', thinking the trap points had gone over and that he was about to get the road. On one occasion, a trainman thought he *was* hallucinating when he happened to casually glance out of the cab window and see a complete forearm with an attached hand lying on the ballast. Expecting to see other parts of a mannequin scattered around, and failing, the grim realization suddenly hit him. Just around the corner from Sunnyhill was Peartree station, a notorious spot for vandalism – and suicides.

Stud Farm Revisited 1993-94

By the end of 1993, the job changed yet again, with a return to Stud Farm. There were still two jobs running, but for us, they no longer originated from Doncaster or Healey Mills. The jobs were now trip workings starting from Derby. The 93 trip (T93) had a signing on time of 07:00 and was light loco off the shed to collect the empty train from either Chaddesden or Sandiacre. The 91 trip (T91) was revived, and with a new signing on time of 09:15, also had a similar diagram to T93. Most of the empty trains were collected from Sandiacre and departed by the high-level goods line to Leicester. After which, it was the usual run round at Knighton and strenuous climb up to Stud Farm. With the job returning via Leicester and straight into Toton by the high-level again, it only remained for the train crew to propel and secure the wagons in Sandiacre, before returning light loco to Derby and a generally reasonable finish – the job had finally come full circle. It was the same for me too, Cliffe Hill had been my first job as a new trainman, and now, in 1994, with redundancy inevitable, Stud Farm became my last.

9. THE YORK TANKS

When you spent most of your time on the largely unglamorous local shunt and trip work, a run to York with a potentially dangerous cargo was quite an adventure, and a brief elevation in status. I enjoyed working the York Tanks for several reasons, primarily because it was a brakevan job and they were a real novelty for a modern-day trainman. Once ensconced in your little home from home at the rear of the train, you were your own boss. You could stand out on the veranda in summer and watch the world go by or cosy up to a nice hot stove in winter. For me, it was proper, traditional railway work, but work that was all too quickly disappearing.

Riding in a brakevan, as opposed to a loco cab, was a truly unique experience. Unique because when you were in the cab, everything was in front of you and ultimately heading your way, but in a brakevan, you saw everything in review, or perhaps more appropriately, retrospectively. It's hard to explain fully, but for me, a deeper familiarity with a route would develop, purely from the raw motion of the brakevan. You felt closer to the track and therefore shared a greater connection to it, more so than in the cab. As many of the old-hand guards could attest to, it was perfectly possible, even if blindfolded, to know exactly where you were on a route, just by the feel of the train on the track; different speeds and gradients, movement over junctions, noises the wheels made, even trackside smells all gave a clear indication of your exact location. Every bump and lurch meant something. All these sensations were obviously perceptible from the cab, but to a lesser degree. The brakevan added a unique atmosphere and the only way to recreate that up front would be to have a steam engine pulling the train. I also found the journey to York via the 'old road' fascinating, which added to this feeling of nostalgia. There was much industry, past and present, to be observed along the way, all in perfect harmony with the railway. But most of the people and places had, or were about to be, consigned to the history books, and much of our way of life was destined to suffer the same fate.

Designated 6E70 and headed by a Class 47, the train normally consisted of twelve chlorine tanks, with a barrier wagon at each end and the inevitable brakevan bringing up the rear. The job originated from Bescot and its destination was the ICI plant at Wilton, near Redcar. The Derby driver and guard signed on at 12:56, relieving a Bescot crew at Platform 1. As soon as the guard was aboard, it was important for him to take possession of the train list. This identified the hazardous material(s) being conveyed, the individual wagons, an emergency telephone number, and finally, the necessary signed authority for the train to proceed. The stove would already be glowing, regardless of the season, but a wise guard would wait until the train was under way before putting his mash can on to boil. Even so, during any brakevan journey, a can full of water could be rapidly reduced to a thimble full, particularly with a rough driver. Once the signalman had given the road, the guard would show his green flag to the driver and await the inevitable lurch on departure. This of course, was the textbook method of departing a station, which didn't always correspond to real life, especially when a certain guard, renowned for his talkative ability, was paired with a driver whom, because of his intense dislike of overtime, was permanently in a rush to get home...

As the relieving Derby crew walked down the platform towards the train, the brakevan would be encountered first so, on arrival at the loco, the driver could safely assume that the guard was aboard and had been for several minutes. Ordinarily this assumption would be correct, but one day, as the previously mentioned duo made their way along the platform, the guard espied the station master and proceeded to engage him in some lengthy dialogue. The driver meanwhile, already in a hurry to get done, continued to the loco and climbed into the cab. Realizing he had been given the road, he immediately opened the power handle and got underway. The guard was still engrossed in his conversation, but on seeing the black exhaust plume issue from the distant loco, he suddenly realized he was meant to be elsewhere. Quickly bidding the startled station master farewell, he ran after the now rapidly departing brakevan and literally threw his bag and himself onto the veranda. As the train disappeared over Derby North Junction, the station master was left scratching his head, no doubt pondering the manner of such men.

Northbound from Derby, the first tunnel on the route was Milford, situated between Duffield and Belper. You knew it was coming, but it still came as a shock to be suddenly plunged into complete darkness, save for the comforting glow of the stove. At 855 yards, it was long enough to be disorientating, so this was a good time to ascertain the exact whereabouts of your Bardic hand lamp. After Belper station, the train might be turned in at Broadholme Loop to allow an express past, or a passenger service to either enter or exit the Matlock Branch, but with the picturesque Derbyshire countryside as a backdrop, there were worse places to be held. The open countryside also offered a brief interlude before encountering the next major tunnel at Clay Cross. At 1 mile, 24 yards, this was a real black hole, and whenever I travelled through it in a brakevan, I always wondered what it would be like to get stuck in there – until one day it happened. On that occasion, the train was about halfway through when I became aware of the brakes being applied. That wasn't unusual, particularly since Clay Cross Junction was the next point after clearing the tunnel, but as a rule, this job didn't encounter many red signals. For some strange reason, most signalmen were keen to pass us on as quickly as possible. My eyes hadn't yet adjusted to the darkness, but fortunately I'd kept my Bardic close at hand and shone it on the wall where the emergency air brake and gauge were situated. This was obviously no ordinary brake application, as the needle continued its rapid descent to zero and we finally came to a juddering halt. As there was no means of communication with the driver, it could have been an emergency application for all I knew, but from the evidence, I suspected that his foot had momentarily slipped off the DSD pedal. Nevertheless, it was serious because as we were carrying dangerous

58

goods, the rules now dictated that I immediately apply a track circuit clip (a length of wire with a metal clip at each end) to the adjacent running line and stop the job completely. When placed on each rail of the track, the clip acts like a wheel and axle combination of a train and causes a short circuit, giving the impression that that section is occupied, thus putting the signal in the rear to danger. I grabbed a clip and was just contemplating a dark and perilous trek in the tunnel with my detonators, when I heard the air building up again. It was fortunate that I hadn't yet alighted the brakevan because as soon as the gauge needle hit 72.5 psi, the train lurched clumsily off again. Apparently, I had weighed up the situation correctly, but I think the driver removed a couple of years from my life expectancy that day.

At Clay Cross Junction, the train would be switched onto the Down Goods, passing the large coking plant at Avenue before crossing the London Midland/Eastern Region boundary at Horns Bridge. The plant at Avenue reinforces my earlier statement about trackside smells. With its thick, sulphurous atmosphere, there was little doubt that you were somewhere between Clay Cross and Chesterfield. The crooked church spire at Chesterfield also provided an unmistakable landmark as the train bypassed the station and continued through Tapton Junction towards Barrow Hill. Lines of drab HAA coal hoppers filled the sidings there, sullenly awaiting their next merry-go-round (MGR) trip – a respite from their relentless journey of colliery to power station to colliery again. After a quick glimpse of the depot roundhouse, the train would continue past Renishaw Park Colliery and Orgreave Coking Plant before encountering Treeton Junction. On rare occasions the train could be diverted here, to pass through the vast, but now largely derelict Tinsley Yard. However, as a special order was required beforehand to divert any dangerous goods trains, there were generally few surprises to be had. The main industry would then briefly switch from coal to steel, as the train progressed through Rotherham Masborough and the complicated looking Aldwarke Junction, before coal returned with a vengeance. Manvers, Goldthorpe, Hickleton, Frickley and South Kirby collieries lay amongst four small provincial stations, after which came the rather grim looking platforms of Pontefract Baghill. Ferrybridge Power Station would now be in sight, and once in the shadow of the cooling towers, the guard would usually acknowledge a wave from the signalman there before the train rumbled over the River Aire and immediately into Brotherton Tunnel towards Milford Junction. Occasionally you would catch a glimpse of the large coal barges on the river, carrying out much the same duties as the MGR trains, but perhaps in a more majestic manner.

After Milford Junction came Sherburn-in-Elmet, Church Fenton and Ulleskelf stations, or as one old-hand guard used to refer to them: German in a helmet, Shane Fenton and Ukulele. Industry now gave way to more open country once again, and on a nice clear flying day, several Jet Provost aircraft could be spotted in front of the hangars at RAF Church Fenton. Around this point the track began to sweep round in a lengthy curve, so it was possible to look back from the veranda and see another train following behind in the next but one section. This could be a little unnerving, especially when you spent most of your time up front in a cab, never really considering what was happening behind, but you had to assume the signalman knew what he was doing. After Ulleskelf came Colton Junction with its high-speed crossover, where a HST could switch from one main line to another without slowing. The train was now well on the approach to York, and after passing the largely empty Dringhouses and Holgate sidings, the unmistakable canopied station would be in sight, with the Minster in the background. To bypass the station, the train would be signalled into York Yard South, where a Thornaby crew would relieve the Derby driver and guard. The Derby men would then make their way across the tracks to the station, to catch the next passenger train home – or back on the cushions, as it was often referred to. With the crew arriving back in Derby around 20:00, it was a satisfactory conclusion to an efficiently run job, before the impending, but inevitable changes.

Although Derby didn't really play a part in the return working of the tanks, there were often instances when it was diverted, and we were thus called upon to conduct Bescot crew via Leicester and Nuneaton – a laborious, roundabout journey to be sure. The timings for this trip weren't too appealing either, as the Derby crew were required to sign on duty at 02:12. No matter how often I worked these unnatural hours, I never got used to them. Walking into the mess room at that time in the morning felt more like a dream than reality. Spare men would view you cautiously with half open eyes. The odd grunt of acknowledgement or enquiry as to your destination might be forthcoming, but once it had been established that you were neither threat nor benefit to them, they would return to their partially comatose state.

The job would eventually arrive in the station, and after greeting our respective Bescot counterparts, I would give a green lamp from the brakevan indicating that we were clear to depart. First it would be the usual uneventful trip out to Leicester, passing the all too familiar Knighton loop, then the train would virtually turn back on itself at Wigston Junction and head along the South Leicester Line. At most times, I considered this to be a largely uninteresting stretch of track, but at that time of the morning, it was especially dark and nondescript. Apart from Croft Sidings situated between Narborough and Hinckley, things didn't really become exciting until we reached Nuneaton Midland Junction. At this point, we were often routed high-level over Nuneaton station. There would be a brief sensation of mid-air flight as it passed beneath us, before encountering the box at Abbey Junction, where the signalman was keeping his lonely vigil. After Nuneaton came Arley Tunnel, but its approaches were naturally gloomy, even during the day, so only the increased draught and change in air pressure indicated that you were passing through it. This was the difference between day and night travel in a brakevan. During the dark hours, the senses were dulled, and the monotonous motion was sometimes disorientating. With every unexpected bump or lurch, the Bescot guard would glance in my direction and I would try to look confident that I knew exactly where we were on such a dark, indistinguishable track. Our roles would be reversed however, once we encountered the vast expanse of Sutton Park. After the tunnel, Daw Mill Colliery and sidings would be passed, before the train emerged at Water Orton. From there, it was turned across to Sutton Park and Walsall.

After working its way round Pleck Junction, the train would finally enter Bescot and the Derby crew would alight at the loco holding sidings. There were often several rows of idling Class 31s stabled here, all belching out thick, choking diesel fumes. After emerging from the brakevan, bleary-eyed and experiencing symptoms akin to severe jet lag, this sweet, sickly cloud really completed the wretchedness of your condition. The first passenger train arrived at Bescot Stadium station around 06:00, so there would perhaps be time for a cuppa before heading to Birmingham New Street and the interminable journey home. There was one small 'bonus' from these trips, I eventually added Bescot to my road card.

Life in the brakevan – a home from home, March 1992. *Author.*

10. ON THE DENBY

"Who's on the Denby then?"
That was the question usually echoing around 4 Shed mess room about 12:15 on a weekday. I think it was asked more out of panic than actual interest, because if someone didn't show up for it between then and 12:30, things didn't look too promising for anyone unfortunate enough to be sitting spare, and who signed the road. It was a relief then, when the designated crew did show up. People expecting to be landed with the job could relax and make fun of the chosen three who would have to tackle the branch once again.

I remember the 'Denby' being largely unpopular amongst the Derby trainmen, but to a couple of us at 4 Shed, it was what working on the railway was all about. Within its diagram, you had all the essential elements of proper railway work. People went to great lengths to avoid it, which always seemed strange to me, as they missed out on the enormous entertainment value the branch had to offer. What true railwayman could resist collecting a staff and running 36 empty HAA wagons and two brakevans up a five-mile single line branch, negotiating no fewer than seven trainman operated (TMO) crossings, performing a unique shunting operation and then returning with about 1,000 tonnes of power station coal? To further complicate matters, standing orders required that all this had to be accomplished before darkness, fog or falling snow. Not always an easy task when signing on duty at 12:22 during the winter months, especially if the job was already running late. Of course, traversing the branch was only one part of the job. The train would then have to proceed to Willington Power Station to unload, before returning to Toton via the Stenson Branch. The empties would be propelled into the Old Bank Sidings and the loco (usually a pair of Class 20s), left on the fuel line. Even then, it wasn't over for the Derby crew, as it was often a mad dash for the 19:25 staff minibus to Long Eaton station, to catch the next train back to Derby – that's if you were running to schedule. Perhaps that was why the job was never well received?

As the crew were signing on, the first of two questions was always asked of the TCS; "Is it running?" A nod of the head, often accompanied by a sadistic grin, would then immediately elicit the second question; "Where is it?" As the train originated from Toton, it was unusual for there to be any substantial delay, so after 40 minutes or so, the TCS would phone through to the mess room to inform the crew that it was waiting for them on the

Down Goods. Whilst the driver and secondman had to trudge all the way along Platform 6 to the north end of the station to access the loco, the guard was able to climb into the brakevan straight away, as it sat almost on the staff foot crossing between Platform 6 and the mess room. On relieving the Toton men, the secondman and guard would ensure they had obtained a two-way radio and a crossing gate key apiece, a radio check would then be made, and the signalman informed that they were ready for the off.

On one occasion, we had to collect the train from St Mary's Down Reception, which was roughly half a mile down the line, but as Big Bill, our driver was of the portlier persuasion and not keen to walk that far, we managed to scrounge a lift from a colleague who was signing off duty. He dropped us in West Meadows Industrial Estate and we had to scramble up an embankment to reach the track. Big Bill however, was unable to negotiate this obstacle by himself, so whilst I endeavoured to pull him up, our secondman had his shoulder firmly wedged against his backside and was rather ungracefully shoving him up. I think it was the only time where an actual driver had required banking assistance. (A loco that pushed or pulled a train up a steep gradient was called a banker, hence banking assistance.)

Once in the brakevan, the guard would first check the status of the fire, then a quick glance to ensure the necessary safety equipment was aboard, and maybe even a read of the latest graffiti whilst waiting on the signalman. Had anyone new made the Denby Hall of Fame? Membership was exclusive; you had to knock a gate down to qualify. (That being the case, I think I ended up slightly over qualified!) If the driver was in a good mood, he might warn the guard that they were about to depart. Nevertheless, the guard would soon hear the unmistakable, and awful, metallic clang of the couplings as they stretched out between wagons, starting from the loco and building up to a violent crescendo along the length of the train. BANG! The brakevan would immediately be yanked from a standstill to about 15mph and anything not held securely in place would fly into the air. Essential tea making equipment, such as the mash can and mugs, previously benign objects, would suddenly become hostile projectiles.

It was always fun to have a new starter initiated in the ways of the brakevan, as they would be invited to sit down with a generous cup of tea, perhaps even begin to prepare a roll-up, only to wonder what this terrible clanking noise was rapidly heading their way, and why the other person was firmly wedged in a corner. The moment of realization would eventually dawn, but it was always too late. The tea would be slopped, the tobacco would be flung over the shoulder and the head would involuntarily make contact with the wooden panel wall. Many a curse was relayed to a driver by the radio after a rough departure.

On departure from Derby, the train would continue along the Down Goods for about three miles before reaching Little Eaton Junction, and the start of the Denby Branch proper. The train could be held here, sometimes for an indeterminate length of time, as Toton often ran a morning job and could still be occupying the branch. At peak efficiency with the rapid loader in operation, three trains a day were run along the branch, the first two operated by Toton. Also, the train would have to await a path across the main lines, so any Derby man departing north on a passenger service would recognise the job with its unique formation of a brakevan at each end, realize it was being held for him and ultimately whistle 'arseholes' as he shot past. (Using the two-tone horn, this was achieved by a short blast of the high note then a long blast of the low note, in case readers were wondering.)

Eventually permission would be given to proceed onto the branch, where the first set of gates would be encountered at Little Eaton Station Crossing. More importantly, that was where the staff had to be collected and given to the driver, firstly to give us protection to travel along the single line branch, and secondly to unlock the ground frame at Kilburn – essential for the train's return journey. There were stories of a secondman who once forgot to collect the staff, a serious error, but even worse when he found he was unable to operate the ground frame. Fortunately, there was a regular bus service that runs parallel to the branch, and thus, a rather annoyed driver dispatched him to retrieve the vital staff.

Once the staff was aboard, and the secondman had opened the gates, the train could proceed through towards the next set at Little Eaton Village Crossing. There was barely a train length between these two crossings, so at this point, the rear of the train would be still be foul at Station Crossing. You could almost read the minds of the waiting motorists as the guard made his way towards the gates. The train has stopped; the guard is walking up, what's wrong? Eventually the secondman would open the gates at Village; I say eventually because these gates had been hit so many times that they would only open in a certain order. The train could then continue through, only to be stopped almost immediately whilst the guard closed Station Crossing. The trick for the guard then of course, was to accurately judge when to stop the train. If insufficient distance had been left between the rear of the train and the now closed gate, there may be enough slack in each wagon coupling for the train to set back by a couple of wagon lengths. The result being one red-faced guard, a few worried motorists and some freshly produced firewood.

Once the guard had secured Village Crossing, the train would then have a reasonable run to the former station at Coxbench and its two pairs of gates. Two roads merged into one at that point, and both on practically blind bends. Although the road wasn't generally fast or busy, it wasn't uncommon to hear a squeal of brakes from an unsuspecting motorist suddenly encountering a gate across their path. After Coxbench, the train would proceed around the corner to Holbrook Crossing. There would be just enough clearance for the guard to secure Coxbench gates before the secondman opened Holbrook, thus minimising the delay to road traffic. Once Holbrook Crossing had been successfully negotiated, it would be a nice steady climb for a mile, then under the A38 bridge before rounding the corner for the approach to Kilburn Crossing.

The two pairs of gates at Kilburn spanned a busy road and were possibly the most daunting on the route. A degree of patience was required to wait for a suitable gap in the traffic before swinging them out. On one occasion, a new trainman learning the job hadn't reckoned with the speed of the traffic. He swung one of the gates out, causing a car to brake violently. The car managed to stop but another one ran straight into the back of it. The train continued through regardless, and when I arrived on the scene in the brakevan, it had developed into a three car pile up. I'd rarely seen so much devastation. Fortunately, no one had been hurt, so whistling innocently to myself, I quickly secured the gates and caught up with the rapidly departing brakevan.

The train would continue past the bunker and up through Denby North Crossing, passing the loaded wagons for the return journey. Once in the run round loop, the guard would uncouple the rear brakevan. The train would then proceed over Street Lane Crossing and into the head shunt, until the last wagon had cleared the sidings head points. The guard would pull the hand points and call the train back, dropping the first three wagon handbrakes. Once the first road of the sidings had been filled, the bunker operative would uncouple, the guard would send the train forward, set the points for the next road and call the train back again. The wagons would normally be accommodated in the sidings within two or three of these movements. Street Lane Crossing would be secured, the guard would uncouple the loco with the remaining brakevan, set the points and propel it into the run round loop to couple up with the other one. The loco would then run round the brakevans, and once re-coupled, draw them both back through Denby North, to a point roughly 50 metres away from Kilburn gates, where the rear brakevan would be uncoupled. The loco and remaining brakevan would continue forward through Kilburn gates again, until clear of the ground frame, where the secondman would change the points and set them back onto the fully loaded train. (A dizzying paragraph but think how it was for the poor train crew.)

If the guard was thinking ahead, he would bank the fire in his original brakevan (the one now behind the loco) and put a can of water on the boil. This would be his residence once more after running round at Willington Power Station. Also, a quick trip to the nearby shop would be in order, for a pasty to warm on the stove – and the usual pork pie for Big Bill. After examining the loaded wagons, calculating the driver's slip, and performing a brake test, the train would be ready for departure – and this is where the fun would begin...

Once the rear of the train had cleared Kilburn gates and the secondman had reset the ground frame, the guard was required to roll his brakevan onto the back of the train. It sounds easy, but it took a bit of skill to judge exactly. There was little room for error, as the results could be extremely embarrassing, particularly with several motorists as an audience. The basic theory was for the guard to release the handbrake just enough to get the van rolling, thus allowing the gradient to take over, whilst continuing to gently rub the brakes. The van would then trundle merrily over Kilburn

Crossing, to arrive at the rear of the train totally under control and ready to couple up. I've witnessed both extremes of this manoeuvre, ranging from the nervous guard who releases the handbrake, only to re-apply it too soon and come to a dead stand on the crossing, to the deranged guard who releases the handbrake with total abandon, only to hurtle over the crossing, hit the buffers of the last wagon and bounce back over the crossing, much to the amusement of the waiting motorists. In each case, with not quite enough gradient to get the brakevan rolling again, and too embarrassed to ask the driver to set back a little, you wouldn't think someone could push a 21-ton brakevan, but it was done on a few occasions. Once re-coupled, the secondman would retrieve the staff from the ground frame and help the guard secure Kilburn gates, before returning to the loco.

May 1991 saw the introduction of a rapid loader, making the whole operation a lot more efficient by rendering Street Lane Crossing, the sidings and all the intensive shunting obsolete. On arrival at Denby, the loco (now usually a Class 56) would be set on slow speed and the empty wagons simply drawn through the rapid loader, under instruction from the bunker operative. The secondman would still open Denby North gates, but only at the last minute, as the train made its snail-like progress towards Street Lane and the end of the line. When opened, Denby North gates obstructed a quiet backwater lane, which served barely a handful of houses. There were perhaps four cars up and down all day, but as soon as the secondman opened the gates, one would suddenly appear, pushing to get across. It was the scene of several heated arguments, as one resident motorist just couldn't understand why he wasn't allowed to cross in front of the train as it continued its slow, but nevertheless relentless plod barely a car length away from him.

Whilst languishing in the brakevan, the guard would probably use this time to prepare a driver's slip and put the all-important can of water on the boil, before transferring his belongings into the brakevan nearest the loco – if not already summoned to participate in an argument at Denby North that is. Whilst walking up, he would be able to give the wagons a cursory examination, as the bunker staff tended to grossly overfill them.

Once loading had been completed, the guard would set the hand points and ride in the rear brakevan whilst the train set back through the rapid loader onto the adjacent road. Although the thrill of rolling the brakevan onto the train was no more, this manoeuvre sometimes had its moments, as about 1000 tonnes of coal could be a tricky load to handle downhill, especially on wet rails. With a foot crossing and then the trap points looming, it was a sensible guard who had one hand on the emergency brake and one foot on the step board ready to 'bail out', particularly if the train was showing no sign of slowing, or even worse, beginning to slide. Once in clear, the loco would be run round, ready for departure.

The revised workings brought a new signing on time of 11:47 for the Derby crews. A strange practice of having assisting trainmen was introduced towards the end of 1992. From successfully operating the branch with just the driver, secondman and guard, there were suddenly two additional trainmen to 'assist' with the gates. This was supposed to improve health and safety, and having more people was supposed to mean fewer accidents, but on this job, the results were often the opposite. As none of the gates had lights on them, or any sort of advanced warning for motorists, the reasons for not using the branch during darkness, fog or falling snow were understandable. However, it was rare for the job to arrive at Derby so late that it couldn't be run up the branch in the daylight, but if, on arrival at Denby, conditions had deteriorated to a point where the train could not return, it would be left there until the following day and the crew would return light loco and an early finish.

On one occasion, the fog did descend on the approach to Denby and an unfortunate trainman had an unexpected appointment with the resident nurse. The gates would be opened for the train and often just secured with a chain. However, a strange phenomenon would sometimes occur on the Denby Branch, whereby a gate would somehow release itself and fold in towards the train under its own weight. On this occasion, it happened just as the rear brakevan was about to clear Kilburn gates. The secondman was one side, the assisting trainman was the other and the guard was on the brakevan – so far, so good. Unfortunately, the guard, thinking he was almost clear, had decided to stand on the step board, not expecting one of the gates to suddenly swing out of the gloom and clip his knees. His scream tailed off into the fog as the train cleared the gates. The two trainmen, thinking they'd seriously injured him, caught up with the brakevan and tentatively peeked inside. They were greeted by the sight of the guard, handkerchief in one hand, cigarette in the other, sitting with his trousers rolled up, exposing two rather skinned knees. If he'd knotted the handkerchief and put it on his head, he'd be perfect for Skegness beach. The trainmen had to quickly close the door and stifle a laugh, before entering seriously. The first words uttered by the guard proved he was okay, "I'm claiming my rest day!" It was suggested that he visit the nurse, so he hobbled off in the direction of the bunker. A short while later, another fog-piercing scream was heard as the nurse liberally applied iodine to his raw knees. All in all, it was not a happy day for him.

The same guard always wore the double-breasted uniform jacket, which had a pen pocket on the inside. After securing Kilburn gates once, he inadvertently put the padlock key into this pocket. The pocket obviously had the same dimensions as a pen, but unfortunately his hand didn't, so it was impossible to retrieve the key. The waiting motorists looked on in amazement as he spun around, rather like a dog chasing its tail, two fingers jammed into this pocket trying to retrieve the key. The nurse very nearly accosted him again as she considered it to be a serious affliction of some sort, the only cure being another hefty dose of iodine.

The Denby phenomenon manifested itself for me one wet, grey December afternoon in 1991, as we made the return journey along the branch. I was the guard on this occasion and was residing in the brakevan, attempting to get dry after each crossing. The train was halfway through Village Crossing when I decided to stick my head out to check our progress.

I thought I was imagining things at first, but it suddenly dawned on me that the right-hand gate wasn't secured properly. It flapped casually back and forth, almost mockingly, as each wagon passed. I was silently urging the train to speed up, so we'd get through before it encountered one of them, but it was not to be. I watched helplessly as the gate finally connected with a passing wagon. There was a terrible splintering of wood as it reared up and snapped in half like a twig. I duly jumped off the brakevan as it cleared the crossing, trying not to look at the rather white-faced motorist who was at the front of the queue. He sat looking at me open mouthed as I removed the debris from the road and his car bonnet.

"It saves me having to open them for you doesn't it," I said cheerily, before retreating to the brakevan to contemplate yet another report form. There was a small bonus to be had from this mishap; there was no shortage of wood for the brakevan stove for a while.

Readers might think there would be plenty of fuel for the stove on a coal train, but power station coal is extremely fine and completely useless on a normal fire. You also had to make sure the brakevan door nearest the last wagon was closed, particularly on a hot summer's day, as once up to speed, the forward motion of the train would funnel all the fine particles in your direction. You could hear them hitting the plastic windows like rain, permeating everything. You might as well have just spent a shift down the pit and be done with.

Once off the branch, the approach to Derby could often be entertaining, particularly if there were assisting trainmen aboard. They were now surplus to requirements and would be anxious to disappear at the earliest opportunity, passing on their timesheets, to be completed and handed in by the remaining crew. We were often routed through Platform 2, obviously non-stop, so anyone 'bailing out' from the loco would stand ready in the doorway whilst the driver slowed and checked the windows of Wyvern House for any management (real or imagined), who happened to be looking out. Once the all clear had been given, departing train crew would develop a sort of clockwork style run/walk, as they exchanged a moving train for a stationery platform. If the same crew was booked on the job all week, arrangements would be made so that everyone had an early day at least once, providing the people remaining with the job had the necessary road knowledge. When Class 56s became the regular traction on the job, some Derby drivers weren't familiar with the loco and so required a conductor driver to ride with them for a time. This was the scenario one day as we rolled down Platform 2. It must have been a Friday because everybody wanted an early finish. The assisting trainman quickly departed, closely followed by the driver, leaving myself as secondman and the conductor driver at the controls. I suppose this would have been okay, except that the conductor driver didn't have road knowledge of Willington Power Station, or the Stenson Branch. Everyone had been in such a rush to leave, that this 'small' matter had been overlooked. I consoled the now worried conductor driver that I knew the route as well as anyone and would talk him through it as we progressed. Even though it was against all the rules, he requested that I drive instead, so I took over from Derby and we completed the job without incident.

About four miles west of Derby, the train would arrive at Stenson Junction, where it would be routed into Willington Power Station. Once the loco had been run round again, the train would proceed through the bunker on slow speed to unload. As the wagons were drawn through, their doors opened automatically, dropping the coal onto a belt beneath, where it would usually be conveyed to a large outside storage pile. The guard would change brakevans for the last time, no doubt glad there was a can of boiling water and a nice warm pasty waiting for him, particularly if it was a dark winter evening. Although the fire gave some illumination, I often took a candle as well, making the brakevan almost a home from home, ready for the journey up the Stenson Branch to Toton.

It is roughly thirteen miles from Stenson Junction to Sheet Stores Junction via the branch, passing Castle Donnington Power Station and through Back Lane Crossing, before eventually passing under the M1, over the River Trent and rounding the corner for Lock Lane Signal Box. One dark November night, it was my turn for an early finish and through earlier arrangement with the secondman, it was decided that I would alight at Sheet Stores Junction, where it was usual for the train to be held. This was a convenient location for me to get to Long Eaton station, and as I had an assisting trainman still riding in the brakevan with me, I assumed everything would be okay and I could slip away into the darkness. Unfortunately, I didn't consider a very observant signalman at Lock Lane, who reported to Control that the guard had absconded – yet another report to fill in.

Once through Sheet Stores Junction towards Trent East Junction, the train would pass Trent PSB and on towards Toton. The train would continue through Toton centre and past Stapleford & Sandiacre Signal Box, right up towards Stanton Gate, before propelling the empty wagons onto the Old Bank. The loco would be uncoupled, to eventually arrive on the depot fuel line. The crew would then check in with the TCS, hand in the radios and keys and either have a cuppa if they were on schedule or make a mad dash for the staff minibus to Long Eaton station and the next train to Derby, ready to do it all again the next day.

An occasional turf war was fought during the latter days, with Toton men working our 11:47 job straight through, instead of getting relief at Derby. This continued sporadically until we did finally lose the job to them.

Lead (and cover) photo: 56020 approaches Holbrook Crossing, with the author ready to 'bail out' for the gates, January 1992. *Jim Riley.*

11. WASHWOOD HEATH

There was never any mistaking the Washwood Heath job. Two Class 37s hauling 23 heavily laden RMC aggregate wagons, each in their distinctive orange and cream livery. Weighing in at around 2,500 tonnes, it was rivalled only in size and motive power by the Corby-Lakenby steel coil train. It certainly made an impressive sight as it snaked its way into Derby along the goods line. The train originated from Peak Forest and was operated by a Buxton driver, who would be relieved at DY449 by a full Derby crew. Signing on at 14:53 (latterly 14:33), the Derby crew would then work the train to its discharge point at Washwood Heath, near Saltley. If the Cliffe Hill job was the first one to be learnt by a new trainman on the early shift, then the Washwood Heath usually became the second one when he switched to a late shift. Both were regular runners and provided an excellent grounding for the novice.

As the drivers exchanged places, the secondman phoned the signalman to get the road, whilst the guard decided which cab to ride in. Officially he was supposed to ride in the rear cab of the lead loco, but I always favoured the lead cab of the second loco, as this way, I would be facing in the direction of travel and could at least enjoy a bit of the view. I always found it quite thrilling to work the Washwood Heath, either as guard or secondman. It always seemed such an exciting and high-profile job, not to mention the responsibility that came with it. Although it was just another aggregate train, having double-headed Class 37s was the real attraction for enthusiastic trainmen and everyone took notice when you got under way. As the job was booked to travel at 60mph, we were nearly always given a good run by the signalmen. Quite often when I got on the phone they would say, "If you get underway quickly, I'll let you go in front of the express." So, you would tell the driver to get cracking and off we'd go. Unfortunately, on one occasion, just as we were departing Derby, the driver's foot slipped off the DSD pedal and we came to a dead stand on London Road Junction. With a train that size, it took a while to blow the brakes off again, so the driver asked me to phone the signalman and tell him we'd come to a stand. As we were right next to the PSB and had been blocking a main junction for nearly five minutes, he was no doubt fully aware of our situation and very likely doing a jig in front of his panel at that very moment.

Once under London Road Bridge and around the slight curve towards Peartree station, we would sometimes encounter kids playing 'Chicken' on the tracks, particularly during the school holidays. As we rounded the corner one afternoon, there were suddenly about three of them stood in our path. Having only just departed Derby, we were still building up speed, but there was simply no way of stopping in time if one of them happened to stumble. I was the secondman on this occasion and gave them plenty horn warning. Several blasts from such a formidable looking train was enough to make them think twice, and fortunately, they moved in plenty of time.

The next day as we warily rounded the corner, the sun was shining directly on the rails causing a glare, but there was what looked to be a figure crouching or lying prone on the track. Again, I gave plenty of horn blasts, but this time there was no movement. Perhaps some kid had fallen over and knocked himself unconscious? There was a sudden sick feeling in the pit of my stomach, that no matter what anyone did, there was just no way of stopping. The terrible realization that we were going to hit someone was bad enough, but that we were powerless to do anything about it seemed much worse. The driver was just about to apply the emergency brake and hope for the best, when we both realized what it was. The prone figure turned out to be a black bin liner full of rubbish placed strategically between the rails. In the next second, we hammered over it on our way to Burton, but it took a while longer for the sick feeling to go away.

As the train approached Burton, the permanent 50mph speed restriction before the station would set off the AWS horn, which the driver would then cancel before reducing speed accordingly. After the last wagon had cleared station limits, he could then open up again between Branston and Wichnor junctions, providing the train wasn't being turned into Elford Loop. Once through Tamworth and Wilnecote stations, the train would then rattle through Kingsbury Branch Junction, passing the oil terminal and scrap sidings on the left. After Kingsbury Branch came Kingsbury Junction itself, where depending on the mood of the signalman (now Saltley PSB), the train could be routed from the main line and onto the slow line towards Whitacre Junction. This four-mile avoiding route sent the train round past Hams Hall Power Station and Coleshill Sidings, to eventually rejoin the main line at Water Orton station. After that, it would be turned onto the Down Goods at Castle Bromwich Junction, to continue past Fort Dunlop and through the gloom of Bromford Bridge towards Washwood Heath. Finally, the train would be turned onto the RMC siding at Washwood Heath East Junction, coming to a stand just before the hopper house.

As one driver used to remark, the sidings at Washwood Heath were a lot like life. There was an up side and a down side. The Up side was made up of about 27 roads, some of which were the domain of the impressive and extraordinarily long Cartic trains. It was difficult to ignore these seemingly endless trains, which consisted of articulated sets of double decked car transporter wagons (four wagons in each articulated set, but only five bogies per set). These transported cars fresh off the assembly lines at Longbridge and Cowley (Austin Rover) to various holding areas around the country. I always used to keep an eye out for the single decked Comtic wagons, which transported the shiny new Land Rovers, forever hoping that one might come adrift and roll off in my direction. However, we were located on the Down side, which wasn't nearly as exciting. Apart from the RMC discharge road, which also incorporated a concrete sleeper-loading gantry, there were just a couple of through sidings and about three CE roads.

A couple of blasts on the horn would alert the RMC operative to our presence, who would then appear to open the control room and start the conveyor belt. Wagons had to be unloaded one at a time under instruction from the guard, so he would obtain a pair of two-way radios from the control room, handing one to the driver and keeping the other for himself. The locos would then be allowed to proceed through the hopper house and set the first wagon for unloading. On the underside of each wagon were three air operated doors and once these were positioned over the pit between the rails, an airline would be connected to the wagon and the doors opened. The stone would then drop into the pit and onto the conveyor belt below, to be deposited onto its corresponding pile in the adjacent storage yard. The train delivered different grades of limestone, starting with dust at one end of the scale, right up through 5, 10, 20mm, etc, to MOT (Type 1), but their positions in the train were dependent on the original train preparer at Peak Forest. Normally the different grades of stone were kept together in batches (e.g., four wagons of dust, six of 10mm, etc), but sometimes the odd wagon of MOT might pop up unexpectedly, which meant the RMC operative would have to dash into the control room and stop the conveyor belt, before re-setting its tripper to the correct pile.

From the guard's point of view, the radio commands were very simple: Forward, Stop (although most people shouted an enthusiastic Whoa!) and Set back. You hoped not to use the last command too often, as it meant the wagon had overshot. Unfortunately, one trainman was afflicted with a stutter, which became more pronounced under stressful conditions, so his commands for each wagon movement often went thus: "FFForward...SSt...SSt...oh sod it...Set back!" Whenever he was booked as the guard, most secondmen exchanged places with him, as it was the only way to get finished in a timely manner. It would only be through pure desperation by the secondman though, as not many were willing to give up their comfortable position up front, to spend several hours setting wagons in an extremely dusty environment. During the winter months, it could be a bitterly cold environment too, so it was in the guard's best interest to set the wagons correctly first time, every time. Even so, it could take nearly three hours for the train to be unloaded, although a guard with a bit of experience could reduce this time slightly. The train could be sent forward as the previously emptied wagon was still having its last door closed. By the time the driver got the train under way, the airline could be removed and connected to the next wagon. As soon as its first door reached the pit, it could be opened whilst the train was still on the move. Providing the stone was flowing nicely and the driver kept a steady pace, the second and third doors could be opened, resulting in most of the wagon being discharged before the train had to be halted again. This was by no means a recommended method, but it could be an extremely efficient way of unloading the train, providing certain conditions were in the guard's favour; the first being that he was particularly quick on his toes. It also hinged on the wagons containing what the train list said they did and the airline successfully popping off the wagon each time. More than once it got stretched a lot further than it was designed to do, as the guard struggled to pull it off the moving train. Once this level of skill had been achieved, the RMC operative usually left the guard to it, whilst he fired up his mechanical shovel and disappeared into the storage yard to keep his stone piles tidy.

Finally, and with always much relief, the last wagon would be set and the secondman asked to return the radio. After being discharged, the guard would ensure the wagon doors had closed correctly and the airline removed before returning to the loco with the secondman. If the guard was on the ball, he would have already made out a driver's slip on the outward journey, so all that remained would be to hand it to the driver. Permission would then be obtained from the signalman to proceed onto the Down Goods again, and once in position, the guard would uncouple the locos and remain with the train, whilst the driver and secondman continued to Saltley to run round. After the monotony of unloading wagons, running round essentially signified the end of the work and offered a welcome change of scenery. The area around Saltley was often a hive of activity, with the depot and Landor Street Junction on one side and Lawley Street Freightliner Terminal and Saltley PSB on the other. Less than a mile away was Grand Junction, where three busy railway arteries joined just before New Street itself. As it was often dusk by the time the locos were run round, the illuminated skyline of Birmingham provided a stark contrast to the dull, but unmistakable gas holders of Washwood Heath. Before alighting, the guard would have taken a spare tail lamp with him to place on the end of the train, thus saving himself some unnecessary walking. Once the locos had trundled past on their return, there would be a further wait whilst the signalman routed them back onto the train at the other end and the secondman coupled up. Although the guard couldn't see any of this taking place, he would eventually hear the wagon brakes blowing off and observe the couplings stretching out slightly, at which point he would conduct a brake test. Assuming everything was in order, he could then finally return to his chosen cab and settle back for the return journey. As with most jobs, toilet facilities were scarce to non-existent, so to protect their modesty, most train crew would retire to the engine room. One trainman however, learnt never to perform the first call of nature through the radiator grille of a Class 37. Just as he was completing this very necessary task, the radiator fan kicked in, sucking the previous contents of his bladder back all over his trousers.

Once the bright lights of Birmingham and its industrial outskirts had receded, the return to Derby was generally dark and uneventful. The guard sensed the previous landmarks only in his periphery, from his position in the second loco. The brightly lit platforms of Water Orton, Wilnecote and Tamworth flashed past, along with the oil terminal at Kingsbury. The speed restriction at Burton would be registered as a hiss of air and a dull thump, as the driver cancelled the AWS in his cab up front. After the silent, brooding presences of Drakelow and Willington had been left behind, the guard might stick his head out the window at Peartree, just to ensure that the train was being routed into the station for relief and not down the goods line. The latter could involve some delay in being relieved and consequently signing off duty, which was a rather unwelcome development, particularly on a Friday night. After being relieved, the crew could finally return to 4 Shed with the satisfaction that another consignment of Derbyshire stone had been successfully delivered to Washwood Heath.

At this point in my life, I was temporarily residing with my parents in Darley Abbey, which in rough railway geographical terms, is situated between St. Mary's Goods Yard and Little Eaton Junction, (two places now consigned to the history books). Even though the old village is about a mile away from the tracks, train noises were still clearly audible, especially ones that involved two Class 37s. My Dad was familiar with our rough time of arrival back in Derby, and whenever he heard the unmistakable sound of the train powering north towards Duffield, he knew that within the next half hour, I would be stepping through the front door.

As with most jobs after 1992, things changed. A single Class 60 replaced the familiar Class 37s, and for me, the mighty Washwood Heath began to lose its appeal slightly. Not that there was anything wrong with Class 60s. Once their initial mechanical problems had been resolved, they eventually proved to be efficient, powerful locos, but being new they lacked character, charm and individuality compared with the Class 37s. I know there were many people who said the same thing when diesels replaced steam, and now here I am, saying it when diesels replace diesels.

A trainman's other involvement within the confines of Washwood Heath was the occasional working to and from the Metro-Cammell factory (latterly GEC-Alsthom), situated next to the Down side sidings. Signing on at 05:25, a driver and guard would be dispatched light loco to collect a rake of Mark IV coaches, which sometimes had a Class 82 driving van trailer (DVT) tagged on the end. Entry into the factory was achieved by means of an electronic ground frame, like the one at Cliffe Hill. Once the train was ready to depart, it would be drawn straight out and run round. Trains arriving from the Down direction could be propelled in though, provided the trainman kept a watchful eye on the road crossing. It was another one of those places where no one was ever seen using the access road, but on the rare occasion where a train had to propel in, it suddenly became rush hour. Whether delivering or collecting the rolling stock, the train would be routed via Nuneaton and the South Leicester Line, with relief usually scheduled at Leicester.

EPILOGUE

Although I was not aware of it at the time, I think true railway life ended for me on the 5th of April 1992. On this normal, inconsequential day, the London Midland Region ceased to exist and the job I knew and loved began to turn into something I barely recognised. From that point onwards, whether by accident or design, management made the job so unpalatable and unrewarding that, to my mind, it practically amounted to constructive dismissal. I had done everything the railway asked of me, and more, but its new masters were not interested. I continued to fulfil my contract to them, but they were no longer willing or able to fulfil theirs. Subtle changes were initiated that eventually had devastating consequences. Things were taken from us and promises were broken...for me, it was the end of the line.

As the trend continued towards transporting more freight by road, I obtained a HGV1 licence and became a driver in the road haulage industry instead. The irony being that I continued to transport aggregates and wait around in quarries and other associated loading facilities. In fact, I am probably one of the few people who have transported aggregates to and from Chaddesden, Stud Farm and Bardon Hill, both by rail and road. But perhaps one day I might be reconciled with the railway, in its next evolution, a bit further down the line? You can take the man from the railway, but you can't take the railway from the man.

Much as it was – the author shares a laugh with his crew members at Washwood Heath, January 1992. *Masonphenix Collection.*

Lost Lines

A series of articles written between 2015 and 2018, which profile some of Derby's lost lines. All appeared in the *Derby Telegraph* between December 2018 and April 2019.

1. Starting at Zero
2. A Test of Time
3. Spondon Treacle Mines
4. The Last Light
5. Echoes of the Denby Branch
6. Brakevan Rules! (Bonus material)

1. STARTING AT ZERO

There was nothing remarkable about the area between the South Dock and the buffer stops at the end of St. Andrew's No2, aka Economac Oil Siding, except for a change of mileage. Not so much an ending as a beginning, as the count started at zero there for everything heading west from Derby.

Depending on demand, one or two trains a week could arrive at Economac (formerly John Hudson Fuels) during the early 1990s. These usually consisted of twelve 100 tonne tankers hired from BP, although their content could originate from various companies and locations, such as Philips Teeside, Gulf Milford Haven and Shell Stanlow or Immingham. When they arrived, a trainman would be dispatched from 4 Shed to run the loco round, but mainly to assist its driver to position the tankers in the siding.

The siding was an extremely dangerous environment in which to operate, as its walkway was invariably coated in a slippery residue, as well as littered with trip hazards such as hoses, stopcocks and associated pipework. Also, owing to the curvature of the track, the driver was unable to observe any hand signals from the ground and had to propel the tankers in blind. It was a move that had to be conducted at slow speed and I eventually adopted the method (which subsequently became common practice in similar hazardous locations) of partially dumping the air brake on the last tanker, to stop the driver once the train had been positioned correctly. It was still a perilous action on the part of the trainman, but as no walkie-talkies were available or (I believe) allowed, it was the safest way of achieving the objective. Funnily enough, all this unorthodox activity used to take place roughly where the East Midlands Control Centre (EMCC) now proudly sits.

Mentioning safety procedures, trainmen had to make their own way to or from 4 Shed, which meant picking a path across London Road Junction, or at the very least, walking alongside a main line...but they were perfectly safe because they had an orange vest on! If the job were still being done today, a taxi would no doubt have to be engaged to ferry them back and forth.

In a similar vein, during my second evolution on the railway in 2006, I once had to visit a long-established nearby factory to recommend they erect a safety fence, as their rear fire escapes led directly onto the track, albeit St. Andrew's No2 – no one had ever realized until then.

Opposite Economac was the Signal & Telegraph (S&T) Dock, with entry and exit controlled by Atlas ground frame, so named because it was adjacent to Atlas Works and its rather imposing crane. During the 1990s, there was an old Satlink train (ZDV wagons and a brakevan), very distinctive in its red and yellow livery, languishing, or more likely stranded in there. Neglected and forlorn, I think some local ne'er-do-well eventually put it out of its misery by setting fire to the brakevan.

About a decade later, I was part of a trackside maintenance team that had been directed to clear the vegetation around the S&T Dock, primarily to provide a more pleasing outlook from the windows of the newly opened EMCC – a tall order indeed! Like some orange clad Indiana Jones type character wielding a machete, I was half hoping to uncover the remains of the old Satlink train, or better yet, the brakevan stove – it would have made a fine chiminea in my back garden.

Running parallel to the former S&T Dock, but separated by Litchurch Lane, is the departure/arrival for the Carriage Works (now Bombardier). This vast site was rumoured to have 365 sets of hand points; one for each day of the year. As a novice trainman, I once asked for a conductor (someone who signed the road) to assist me in taking a train in there. This was a contentious request, as 4 Shed was only about 200 metres away. I could feel my cheeks reddening with embarrassment as I heard the chosen man moaning and stumbling across the tracks towards me. The effect was complete when we simply moved the train about 100 metres and secured it just inside the gate.

Leaving Economac and the S&T Dock behind, the next feature to be encountered is the white edged platform (or rather white elephant) of Ramsline Halt. Opened in 1990 to ferry the away football fans to and from the nearby Baseball Ground, its success was difficult to gauge as, I believe, only four trains ever officially stopped there. I once had to prepare a train of empty Economac tankers that was stood in the platform awaiting westbound departure, but I don't think that counted as one of the four. It was also another occasion where I had to walk from 4 Shed to the waiting train and, as I wasn't accompanying it, had to walk back again. Derby County relocated to Pride Park Stadium in 1997, but rail access to Ramsline Halt wasn't severed or its track lifted until the Derby Re-signalling Project twenty-one years later.

Milepost 1 stands at London & North Western (L&NW) Junction, beyond which is Peartree station. Owing to numerous suicides over the years, and increased anti-social behaviour, security gates restrict access to its sombre platforms. Left at Melbourne Junction is the freight only Sinfin Branch (see separate article 'On a Roll to Royce's'), with its ghost stations of Sinfin North and Sinfin Central. In fact, with Ramsline Halt, there are three ghost stations all close together, four if you include the semi-ghost station of Peartree, being as only two trains a day call there.

Beyond Melbourne Junction are Sunnyhill Up and Down Goods Loops. During the fuel blockade in 2000, one 'enterprising' local managed to siphon off some fuel from the Economac bound tankers whilst they were stood in the Up goods loop, a bit like, I imagine, the Methylamine train heist in *Breaking Bad*, only not as sophisticated.

The next junction is Stenson, where coal trains could be routed into Willington Power Station. In 1990, eight trains a day from the Derbyshire coalfield were helping to satisfy its enormous appetite for power. Closed nine years later, the site is all but cleared, except for its cooling towers, which still dominate the skyline. Willington was not a true MGR power station, as locos had to be run round before entering the discharge point. As the train passed slowly through, the wagon doors would be opened automatically by 'Daleks', with the coal dropping into an underground bunker and distributed into the plant by conveyor. An old driver used to remark that if the wagons were being unloaded quickly, the coal was going straight onto the stock pile, but if unloaded slowly, it was heading straight to the furnace. It sounded reasonable enough, but I don't know if it was true or not – maybe it was just a story to help break the monotony of MGR work.

Although Stenson Junction was the western limit of the 2018 Derby Resignalling Project, it is worth continuing to North Stafford Junction, where straight on for Birmingham or right for Stoke-on-Trent, will still mean chasing the sunset. Bearing right however, provides an opportunity to consider another lost line at Egginton Junction; the former Mickleover Test Track. I worked one of the last trains on the test track in 1990, only to return as relief signalman at Egginton Junction sixteen years later. The signal box was set to close in 2016 but, at the time of writing, it has yet to fade into the sunset.

Lead photo: Milepost Zero can still be found lurking in the South Dock at Derby station. *Author*.

2. A TEST OF TIME

'The Research and Development Division test line between Mickleover and Egginton Junction is a five and a quarter mile section of the down line of the former [GN] LNER Derbyshire Extension line from Nottingham to Burton and Stafford. The test line is designated "Up and Down" Mickleover line and the direction of line is down from Mickleover to Egginton Junction. Four miles of the former up line which has also been retained is used for purposes ancillary to test movements and is designated "Long Siding".'

The above is taken from the 1974 working instructions, which I recently uncovered in my records. British Rail Research became a separate business unit in April 1989 and subsequently splurged on new structure number plates for most of the over bridges along the line (pictured above). But it would be bridges, or rather the cost of two new ones (A516 and A50 respectively) that would need to be built over the line, that contributed to its closure. Track removal began in September 1990 and, apart from some remnants at Mickleover and a short length at Egginton, was completed about a month later. The former track bed eventually became a section of the Great Northern Greenway (National Cycle Route 54).

The last train

My first trainman job at Derby in 1990 was acting as secondman on an engineering train, headed by 47971 *Robin Hood*, which had been tasked to assist in the lifting of the Mickleover Test Track accessed at Egginton Junction. Therefore, I had the 'honour' of manning one of the last trains (if not *the* last train) on the line – or to clear its Down Stop board anyway. My very first operational job: the removal of track. Not a particularly auspicious start to a railway career.

On that day, the driver, guard and I departed Derby 4 Shed light loco, collected our train from Chaddesden Sidings then proceeded to North Stafford Junction, arriving on the Down Stoke alongside Egginton Junction Signal Box. With the end of our train clear of the trailing crossover, the signalman pulled the points and we propelled onto the Up Stoke. He then reversed the facing points for the sidings and we drew straight in – oddly, there were no ground signals for either of these moves. There were four roads in the sidings then a locked gate across the track for MoD Hilton (closed in 1989). At the time, there were several derelict Class 45s stored in the sidings, which had been used as dead weight loads during Class 60 testing conducted between July 1989 and May 1990. Once our guard had conversed with the signalman, we propelled our wagons past these forlorn looking locos, through the loop, past the 'Beginning of Staff Section' (Up) board and onto the test track proper. I now fully appreciated my role as secondman, interpreting all those hand signalled shunt moves.

When the test track was operational 'One Train Working on Single Lines' applied, and the train staff was coloured black and, unsurprisingly, lettered 'Train Staff'. This was for use between Mickleover and Egginton Junction and was normally kept at Mickleover control centre, but with the appropriate authority, it could be transferred by road to Mickleover, Derby 4 Shed or Egginton Junction Signal Box as required. If it was carried in the loco cab, it had to be shown to the signalman at Egginton Junction, who could not allow a train onto the test track without first satisfying himself that the driver was possession of the correct staff. The maximum speed on the test track was 65mph and 30mph when propelling, subject to certain conditions. Neither train staff nor line speed affected us on the day we arrived with our empty wagons, as there was only a small section of track left to be removed. Therefore, there was very little danger of a collision and certainly no chance of exceeding the speed limit.

We propelled about half a mile to the worksite then, as the remaining track panels were cut and loaded onto our train, we inched slowly forward towards the 'End of Staff Section, Stop and Telephone' (Down) board. Verbal authorization from the Egginton signalman was required for any movements past this board, which was duly obtained. I suppose another train could have been allowed into the loop, but it might not have been advisable considering the ever-decreasing track. Once our train had been loaded, we entered the loop and the loco was run round, enabling us to propel into the sidings and eventually draw straight out onto the Up Stoke back to Derby. There was a ground signal for this move – the only one so far.

Someone became a little overzealous and removed the Up Stoke to sidings connection shortly after. In typical railway fashion, it had to be temporarily re-instated in March 1992, to extricate the derelict Class 45s. The locos were moved to Toton in two convoys. The first, headed by 31271, consisted of 45148, 45126 and 45111; the second, headed by 37222, consisted of 45125, 45146 and 45136. (45136 was not involved in Research work and merely being stored at Egginton.) Apart from 45125 (preserved), the rest were scrapped at M C Metals, Glasgow, that same year. As the trains were unfitted, they each had a brakevan in rear. One of my colleagues – who had not long passed his trainman training – was supposed to be the secondman on one of these jobs but was somehow conned/coerced into undertaking the guard's role. After the event I asked him how it had gone. He admitted that he hadn't been entirely sure what he was supposed to be doing, but the driver had told him "Just get your head down in the brakevan and I'll stand you up when I want you." – such was the 'duty of care' in the 1990s. Thus ended my association with the test track, or so I thought...

Forerunner of the Greenway

After industry privatisation and redundancy from British Rail in 1994, I divided my time between HGV driving and the building trade, primarily groundwork. The following year I got intermittent work with a local haulier, delivering building materials to a new estate that was being built on and around the former MoD land at Hilton. This job sticks in my mind because some of the road names on the new estate retained a military connection, such as Bren Way, Enfield Close, and so forth. In 2000, I helped lay a path on the old track bed from Mickleover (old station) to where the A516 now severed it just before Etwall. Using an old tar-laying machine, we deposited a coarse grade of stone on top of the existing railway ballast to bind it then sealed it with a topping of re-cycled tarmac. If memory serves, we accessed the track bed at Bannalls Lane Crossing (accommodation crossing 21), as this was roughly the halfway point between Mickleover and Etwall – handy for the conveyance of materials in either direction. Stone shouldn't really be run through a tar-layer, but the boss had bought the old machine cheap with the intention of scrapping it after the job. Even with the mechanical assistance, the work still took five weeks – roughly the same amount of time it had taken a PWay crew to remove the track a decade earlier. However, I suppose it was fitting really; I'd removed the track from one end and had now re-surfaced the other. The path eventually became a section of the Great Northern Greenway.

Reflections of a Relief Signalman

No one was more surprised than me when I rejoined the railway in 2006 and ended up as a relief signalman on the North Staffs Line, occasionally working Egginton Junction Signal Box. The 'Junction' part was certainly a misnomer by then, but at one time, its frame had contained 47 levers. It must have been quite an experience to work the box when the Great Northern and North Staffs traffic was all heading your way. The frame now only contained a distant, home and section lever for each direction, plus four spares, a point lever and, unusually, one ground signal lever for Up to Down only – no real change there then! There was also a release lever for the crossing keeper-manned Hilton Crossing. The signal levers operated a mixture of colour lights and cable pull semaphores. On the Up Stoke was a colour light distant, a semaphore home and a colour light section signal. The Down Stoke consisted of a colour light distant, the same for the home then a semaphore section signal. As well as Hilton Crossing and Marston-on-Dove automatic half barriers (AHB), the box supervised three user worked crossings. It was also a fringe box, working Absolute Block to Tutbury and Track Circuit Block to Derby Power Box.

Surveying the scene from the signal box window in 2008 I noted that some of the sidings had been left in situ, although they were now completely overgrown, and more houses had been built around the former MoD land (now Hilton Business Park). I reflected that, not only had I worked one of the very last trains on the former test track (albeit whilst simultaneously removing it), I'd also helped create the Greenway, and had even delivered some of the materials used in the house building. Not content with this potted history and these dubious claims to fame, I once flew over the area in a light aircraft chartered from Derby Airfield at the back of the box; a £25 flight experience where I had been allowed to take the controls. I was only reminded of this brief adventure when being passed for the box. The line manager had asked what steps I would take if an aircraft crashed onto the tracks, "And don't say bloody big ones in the opposite direction!" he had added quickly. Suffice to say that I've viewed the area from a variety of different angles, as well as played a small part in its history – both endeavours that were continuing from my lofty perch in the box. In the future, I will of course expect English Heritage to attach one of those blue plaques to a suitable structure in my honour, if any suitable structures remain that is. Oddly enough, I never got around to walking the Greenway until 2014 but working at Egginton (eventually) inspired me to do so.

The Great Northern Greenway (Mickleover–Egginton Junction)

There are still a few railway remnants to be seen, if you look closely enough. Obviously, it might be better to walk in winter rather than summer, when the vegetation has receded. It is, however, most pleasant to be out there amongst the farm crossings on a summer's evening, listening to the lonely bird cry and watching the sun dip behind the fields. It's not hard to imagine the railway in operation again and its presence is most palpable; ghosts of the Great Northern.

The obvious (still gated) accommodation crossings encountered along the route are Bonehill Farm (20), then Bannalls Lane (21). There is an old red warning board in the undergrowth just before this crossing (possibly an 'End of Signal Section' board), but it has been folded face down and can no longer be read. The next gated crossing is Bearwardcote (22), pronounced Barrowcote. There are remnants of an old signal post in the undergrowth just beyond this crossing, which was very likely MR94; a 4-aspect signal for test purposes only.

There were six accommodation crossings on the line and all must have been challenging when the test track was in use. However, entitled users were advised of any testing beforehand and the gates would be padlocked if access was not required. For test speeds above 45mph, a hand signalman would be appointed at any crossing where an entitled user had requested access.

The track over Heage Lane Bridge (U/B 117) was singled in 1983, leaving the remnants of 'Long Siding' fallow and the Derby/Hilton Road Bridge (O/B 122) has now been nicknamed 'The Pink Bridge', which I imagine would have made a few of the old 4 Shed boys smile.

According to the 1974 working instructions, the usage of accommodation crossing 27 (Massey's) warned of 'cattle twice daily and farm machinery', which could have proved interesting during test days. Fortunately, there was a 15mph permanent speed restriction from here to Egginton Junction in both directions. The old dairy chimney continues to provide a good landmark for the approach to Egginton Junction. I helped remove the remaining track from here to the junction in 1990, but perhaps the powers-that-be are regretting its removal now. It could have formed the first part of a ready-made spur for the Toyota car plant at Burnaston or the proposed railfreight terminal on the adjacent Egginton Common.

As was – the sidings at Egginton Junction in 1990. *Robert Woodman.*

Lead photo: Remarkably, the structure plate for over bridge 115 is still attached to a surviving abutment near Mickleover old station, but the bridge itself is long gone. *Author.*

3. SPONDON TREACLE MINES

"If you don't mend your ways, you'll end up at Spondon Treacle Mines." So went the oft-trotted local admonishment to misbehaving youngsters. It was advice I had obviously failed to heed as, one day in 1990, I found myself second-manning a train of twelve acid tanks that was propelling into the exchange sidings at Spondon Celanese.

Although British Celanese was taken over by Courtaulds in 1957, the works was still commonly referred to as Celanese (a combination cellulose and ease). It was a sprawling 300-acre site (and even had its own power station), but fortunately, as BR train crew, we only had dealings with a small part of it, namely the previously mentioned sidings. However, it was no longer common ground to Derby train crew in 1990, owing to the closure of St. Mary's Goods Yard the year before and the loss of the trip working between the two.

There are numerous historical references and claims to 'treacle mining', but in the case of Spondon, I think it is safe to say that it related solely to the manufacture of cellulose acetate – no doubt someone will correct me on the chemistry, but roughly a mixture of purified cellulose, glacial acetic acid and a catalyst which, when formed and dissolved in acetone, creates a viscous, treacle-like solution for extrusion through spinnerets...so that's what they needed all that acid for.

Cellulose acetate is used in many products, including, no doubt, the filters of the cigarettes our guard was furiously chain-smoking that day as our train set back into the siding. It was my first (and last) time, and he had only been in once before, but the move was simple enough and after the train had been secured in the through siding, the loco was uncoupled, and we returned light to 4 Shed.

There were two (gated) spurs into the plant: south for the power station and acid unloading area, and north for the main plant. Courtaulds used their own locomotives for wagon movements; two Sentinels in two-tone green livery and, up to 1989, a Rushton Hornsby for power station work, with their drivers BR accepted into the exchange sidings.

The site closed in November 2012, with its connection to the main line finally severed during the Derby Re-signalling Project five years later.

4. THE LAST LIGHT

A Mixed Reception

By the time I reported to Derby 4 Shed for trainman duties at the beginning of 1990, railway operations had already ceased at St. Mary's Goods Yard the previous year and my only dealings in that locale were with its remaining Down Reception. Starting roughly one mile north from the station, DY516 signal controlled entry onto it from the Down Main (formerly St. Mary's South Junction) then about half a mile later, DY524 ground position signal controlled its exit onto the Down Goods at St. Mary's North Junction, just under Mansfield Road Bridge.

Not connected to St Mary's, but just across the way was the spur into Thomas Hill's scrap yard (now Sims Metal Management). Derby crews would occasionally propel empty wagons into the sidings from the Up Goods or draw loaded ones out, after first operating a ground frame. The wagons would often be loaded during the night, with the grab operator seemingly dropping the scrap from a great height, which could be heard several miles away. The connection was severed in the 1990s, but the sidings are still very much in situ in what is now called the Parker Centre.

An Unwelcome Reception

We once had to collect our 'celebrated' Denby job (Denby Disposal Point-Willington Power Station) from the Down Reception, as I believe a rather disgruntled Toton crew had abandoned it there several hours previously. (At the time, Toton men were trying to acquire our afternoon trip by underhanded tactics and I gathered that they had departed the station without relief and subsequently been halted in the Down Reception.) However, as Big Bill, our driver was of the portlier persuasion and not keen to walk that far (not much 'duty of care' back then), we managed to scrounge a lift from one of our colleagues who was signing off duty. He dropped us in West Meadows Industrial Estate and we had to scramble up an embankment to reach the track. Big Bill however, was unable to negotiate this obstacle by himself, so whilst I endeavoured to pull him up, Catweazle, our secondman had his shoulder firmly wedged against his backside and was rather ungracefully shoving him up, both constantly bickering with every unsteady step. I think it was the only time in railway history where an actual *driver* had required banking assistance.

Unfortunately, we still had a fair distance to walk, but at least I would access the brakevan first; Big Bill and Catweazle would have to trudge another 36 wagon lengths (38 including the front and rear brakevans), *and* possibly an extra loco length, if a pair of Class 20s were heading the train. Big Bill was not a happy man, and because I had failed to adequately hide my amusement of the situation, I was given a sharp jolt in the brakevan upon our (eventual) departure.

An Unusual Reception

Shortly after, I was the guard on the Denby again and, most unusually, we had relieved the Toton crew in Platform 2 and were now trundling nicely along the Down Main. (Perhaps the signalman wasn't taking any chances with relief this time?) I was just enjoying a contemplative lean on the brakevan veranda when I saw a cow amble across the Up Goods and onto the Up Main. I thought the motion of the brakevan had caused me to hallucinate at first, but after satisfying myself that it was a cow, I pulled the emergency air brake lever, or 'dropped the jigger' as we used to say and stopped the train. Obviously, there were no mobile phones back then (Generation Y would never have survived it!) and the nearest signal post telephone was – yes, you've guessed it – DY516. The conversation went roughly as follows:

"Ey up Bobby, this is the guard off the Denby here, you've got a cow on the Up Main between Derby North and St. Mary's South."

"Yeah right, are you sure it's not a pink elephant?"

"Yep, this has got udders."

"How the hell can a cow get there, it's the middle of an industrial area?" (He had forgotten, or possibly wasn't even aware that the cattle market wasn't far away, and this hapless beast had obviously escaped from it.)

"Well, I don't suppose that area is called West Meadows for nothing," I joked. "Anyway, you'd better stop the job because it was standing on the Up Main the last time I saw it."

The above dialogue wasn't exactly up to today's standard of railway safety critical communications (a mouthful in itself), but he understood the message all right. By this time, the secondman had walked up to see what the problem was – and he didn't believe me when I told him either. We eventually got under way again and I returned to my contemplations on the veranda. However, instead of keeping us on the Down Main, it didn't escape my notice that the signalman turned us onto the Down Goods at St. Mary's North, possibly out of spite for increasing his already busy workload.

An Icy Reception

I was once 00:05 spare (a day shift, but only just) and after kicking my heels for about three hours, was eventually directed by the TCS to accompany a driver who was taking a light loco off the shed. We would be travelling to St. Mary's North, whereupon it would be my job to couple the loco to a train that had been left in the Down Reception, conduct a brake test and then send it on its merry northbound way. When it came to my triumphant return to 4 Shed however, the TCS seemed a little vague, but said he would send the shed men, in another light loco, to come and collect me. I, however, had a better plan. At that time, I only lived about a mile away from the junction, and as I didn't trust the shed men to collect me in a timely manner, or even the TCS to remember to tell them in the first place (it was the depths of winter by the way, freezing cold, snow on ground and so forth), I told him I could walk home from there...after first signing off duty and handing in my timesheet of course. The TCS was notorious for not giving any time away, but *I* was doing *him* a favour, wasn't I, by saving an additional loco journey? After much deliberation and sucking of back teeth, he grudgingly agreed, and the driver and I duly departed. The driver seemed a little concerned about abandoning me in such a spot, and in such conditions, but after his departure, I managed to scramble up the snowbound embankment and clamber over Mansfield Road footbridge parapet. Unfortunately, I made a bit of a clatter during these activities, which set some of the local dogs barking. I was undoubtedly a suspicious character, particularly at 03:30, but my only crime that morning had been to falsify the hours on my timesheet.

As a small aside, after living about a mile away from St. Mary's North Junction for several years, I moved, in 2000, to within 200 metres of it. I moved again in 2011, to house almost directly opposite the former goods shed. Mentioning clattering noises, I suppose the distinctive rattle of the trains over the points will disappear too, after the junction has been remodelled.

A Poor Reception

The driver from the above anecdote didn't have a lot of luck heading northbound. Only recently had he barely survived the wrath of the trainspotters that regularly congregated at the south end of Platform 6. They had been desperately trying to identify a loco tucked away on shed and this driver had been tasked to move it to Derby North Junction and await the return signal. As he rolled off the shed towards the spotters, he decided, rather unwisely, to lean out of the cab window and cover the loco number with his newspaper, thus denying them their prize. With much shouting and shaking of fists, they set off down the platform in hot pursuit, with the driver hoping all the signals were in his favour and that he could keep going. As the loco cleared station, one of the platform staff shouted "Oi, what's all the commotion?"

"The spotters are revolting," came the driver's distant reply.

Well, I suppose there was no argument with that.

(He admitted later that he'd asked the signalman to put him in St. Mary's Down Reception to *eventually* return from St. Mary's North, as Derby North simply wasn't far enough away from the angry mob.)

<u>Old Buffers</u>

The goods yard was redeveloped in 1999 and renamed St. Mary's Wharf. The former goods shed, and grain warehouse are situated on what is now called Prime Enterprise Park, accessed from Mansfield Road, and is home to a variety of businesses, as well as the Coroner's Court. The former railway buildings and new builds in sympathetic style are pleasing to the eye, but I am left wondering why modern railway buildings cannot be constructed so elegantly now. (Incidentally, the former gatehouse and coal merchant's office were removed and 'rebuilt' at Midland Railway Centre.) Turning left off Mansfield Road into Fox Street, a little piece of rail still peeps through the road surface. Turning left again into Clarke Street, the Derwent Business Centre (the former split-level Bonded Stores) still retains a set of buffer stops...on what is now its first floor. St. Mary's Wharf police station and a small housing estate occupy the rest of the former goods yard area.

The track and junctions were remodelled during the Derby Re-signalling Project (North 02 Sep-07 Oct 2018), and the Down Fast now assumes the track bed of the former Down Reception under Mansfield Road Bridge. St. Mary's North Junction has become St. Mary's South Junction, with the former now appearing one mile beyond that.

Lead photo: The last light – that of the title – and the only intact former yard light that remained up to August 2018; one of the few reminders that a yard ever existed. Note its unusual ladder, which bellies out and tilts potential climbers backwards to begin with. *Author*.

5. ECHOES OF THE DENBY BRANCH

"It's not just a job, it's an adventure!"
That was how some of the Derby train crew used to describe working on the Denby Branch...and they were right. The adventure involved running 36 empty HAA wagons and two brakevans along a five-mile single line, negotiating seven trainman operated crossings, performing some unusual shunting manoeuvres then returning with around 1,000 tonnes of coal, all before darkness, fog or falling snow. You would think that alone would have been enough but traversing the Denby Branch was only part of the job. The train would then have to proceed to Willington Power Station to unload, before returning to Toton via the Stenson Branch. Once the empties had been propelled into the Old Bank Sidings and the loco (usually a pair of Class 20s) deposited on the depot fuel line, the crew would then have to make a mad dash for the staff minibus to Long Eaton station and catch the next train back to Derby. On reflection, Mission: Impossible might have been a better description for it some days.

The reason the train had to depart the branch before sundown or inclement weather was because none of its road crossings had any illumination or warning for motorists – unless you counted the simple non-reflective red disc on the gates themselves – the trainman simply swung the wooden gates across the road and hoped for the best. In the current health and safety climate, I doubt this job could even be considered nowadays and, five years post BR, it must have come as a great relief to Railtrack (as was) and the freight operating companies not to have to run trains along it anymore. The job had been reduced to a 'man in a van' following the train, rather than a man in a brakevan during that period anyway.

In BR days however, the branch was operated in traditional style, with Toton running a morning job and Derby an afternoon job. As we worked the last train of the day, it always fell to us to decide whether the loaded wagons could be brought back safely or not. This was never an issue in summer but would certainly become one once autumn rolled around.

Whenever I think of the Denby Branch, I often think of it in late autumn – one of those clear, crisp November afternoons where I am trying to keep my balance on the brakevan veranda as it is inexorably jerked and jolted behind 36 wagons – so it is fitting that I am recreating the journey at the same time of year now, albeit on foot. The branch closed in April 1999 and the track lifted thirteen years later, but its echoes still resonate as I walk along parts of its former track bed now. I heed the advice of one of the last remaining footpath crossing signs. I no longer need to beware of trains, but I do stop, look and listen frequently, and sometimes still hear the squeal of coal wagons, the rattle of the brakevan and the shouts and laughter of the train crew.

The journey really starts at Little Eaton Junction (now Breadsall Junction), just north of Derby. After relieving a Toton train crew in the station yard, we would trundle along the Down Goods for about three miles, before being turned across the main lines at DY536 signal and onto the branch itself. (The connection was severed in 2010, but the signal itself wasn't removed until August 2018 during the Derby Re-signalling Project.) The wagons used to screech pitifully as they were dragged around the sweeping curve towards Little Eaton Station Crossing, no doubt alerting the villagers to our presence once again.

There were stop boards in advance of every road crossing, but few drivers obeyed them, preferring instead to draw right up until the buffers were almost touching the gates. Any miscalculations however, would result in a red-faced driver, a few worried motorists and some freshly produced firewood. The secondman would alight, obtain a walkie-talkie and gate padlock key from the cabin and collect the token from the machine. Well, we always referred to it as the token, but officially it was a one train working staff. He would then open the gates and return to the loco as it continued the short distance towards Village Crossing. Whilst the secondman grappled with Village gates, the rear of the train would still be foul at Station Crossing by about six wagons, so the guard would climb down from his brakevan and collect his walkie-talkie and key. Once radio contact had been established between brakevan and loco, the guard could then stop and start the train accordingly, thus successfully negotiating the train through all the TMO crossings.

There are some sections of the branch now where you wouldn't think a railway had ever existed and I must revert to the road for these first two stages owing to their inaccessibility. (The section from Little Eaton Junction to Village Crossing has largely been built on and/or dense vegetation makes it impassable, but at the time of writing, it was still possible to walk the track bed from Village Crossing onwards.) The traffic at the crossings is just as bad as ever and I am constantly dodging cars whilst trying to take photos. Little Eaton has always had a feel of Olde England about it, the smell of coal fires, its red telephone boxes and an occasional Union flag fluttering in a garden. The villagers, of course, can spot a stranger a mile away and, for some reason, I keep expecting Brian Dennehy to pull up in a sheriff's car and ask me where I'm headed! Therefore, it is with some relief that I cross over Jack O' Darley's Bridge (O/B 3) and temporarily join the track bed towards Coxbench.

The branch is really echoes upon echoes, as the Little Eaton Gangway (officially the Derby Canal Railway) opened in 1795, using horses and wagons coupled in single file, to move coal from Denby to a nearby branch of the Derby Canal at Little Eaton. With the coming of the railway, new track was laid closely following some of the original gangway, and this was extended to Ripley and beyond by 1856. The Ripley Branch, as it was then termed, lost its passenger service in 1930 and its freight by 1968 and the track was subsequently shortened, terminating just beyond Street Lane. Walking along this section now, it is just as easy to imagine horses dragging coal wagons in the 1790s, as it is locos in the 1990s. Both were engaged in the same job, the only real difference between the two being the amount of horsepower involved.

As if the road crossings weren't enough for the train crew, there were also seven footpath and three occupational crossings along the route too. There were three footpath and two occupational crossings between Village and Coxbench alone and because of the meandering track along that stretch, it made them even more hazardous. Although there was a 15mph speed limit on the branch (depending on who was driving), people would occasionally pop up out of the undergrowth, like targets on a shooting range, allowing very little time to sound a horn warning, let alone stop.

I briefly return to the road to get around the old station cottages at Coxbench, as the track bed appears to have been absorbed by several back gardens. Milepost 133 is still in situ but is now just a garden ornament. Although the line closed in 1999, trains could still conceivably run on it (the last being a weed killing train in 2000), but this seemed of little consequence to the residents and their determined encroachment. As I round the treacherous blind bend to Coxbench Crossing, I recall its unusual three-way gate system, owing to two roads merging into one at this point, as well as the squeal of car brakes from unsuspecting motorists having just found said gates across their path.

A little known but perhaps surprising fact is that, during its five-mile meanderings, the Denby Branch traverses the nearby Bottle Brook (or a tributary of it) nine times, which must surely have been the source of a few headaches for Benjamin Outram – founder of the Butterley Company and engineer for the gangway – not to mention George Stephenson (surveyor) and the Midland Railway engineers who followed him.

Perhaps another reason the job had to clear the branch before sundown was the proliferation of lineside pubs along its route: The New Inn and Queens Head at Little Eaton, the Bell & Harp and Fox & Hounds at Coxbench and the Station Hotel (now a crèche!) at Kilburn; not so much a coal job as a pub crawl. With some of the characters I worked with, it was probably wise to get them off the branch before 19:00 because I dread to think what might have happened if we'd had unrestricted licensing hours back then. But perhaps it would have been beneficial for the trainmen to have an alcoholic stiffener at each location; it would certainly have made all that gate opening and closing much easier to bear. I also suspect that is exactly what used to happen on the branch in its early days, as there were also five signal boxes between Little Eaton and Kilburn – one pub for each box – and that's before you even got to Ripley.

I continue along the road to Holbrook Crossing, about 45 HAA wagon lengths away from Coxbench Crossing. Obviously, the train fitted comfortably between the two, so after the guard had closed one, the secondman would open the other, thus causing the minimum disruption to road traffic. As it was now a steady climb from Holbrook to Kilburn, it was natural for a driver to open up for the incline, but very easy to forget that the train would have to stop again for the guard to close Holbrook gates behind it. I was once acting as the guard on a trip where, unbeknown to me, the secondman had been given control of the loco – it only dawned on me after I'd been thrown round the brakevan stovepipe for the fifteenth time. Of course, he made the previously mentioned error and dragged me through Holbrook Crossing at a vast rate of knots. By the time I'd managed to stop him, with several rather terse radio commands, I was a train length away from the gates. I decided not to ask him to set back as I didn't want to test his driving ability any further – we would probably end up seesawing over the crossing for evermore – so I walked back instead, much to the bemusement of the waiting motorists.

I rejoin the track bed just after Holbrook Crossing. This stretch to Kilburn is the most walker-friendly bit, which is surprising, given that it crosses open fields – I was expecting a return of impenetrable vegetation. I'm glad because I always thought this to be the most rail-friendly part of the branch too – a respite from the crossings where you could take in the scenery, or retreat to the shelter of the brakevan and warm your hands against the comforting glow of the stove. The seemingly indestructible old brick PWay cabin (aka Ken's Shack) is still in situ and largely unchanged, apart from the graffiti. Next comes the elegant span of Strutt's over bridge, right before the extremely inelegant span of the A38 over bridge (O/B 10A). I can still hear the clickety-clack of the train reverberating off these structures as I walk through, and an oily, diesel, coal aroma remains in the latter.

Once under the A38, Kilburn Crossing becomes the focal point, and although I'm on foot, approaching it now still gives me butterflies. I can see the cars flashing over the crossing in the distance and remember how I seemingly used to take my life in my hands when swinging the gates across. Dodging the traffic once more, I cross over the busy road and head up towards the remnants of Denby Disposal Point.

The empty train would pass the loaded wagons for the return journey and continue through Denby North Crossing. Once in the short loop between there and Street Lane Crossing, the guard would uncouple his brakevan then the train would continue over Street Lane and into the headshunt, until the last wagon had cleared the sidings points. He would then pull the hand points and call the train back, dropping the handbrakes on the first three wagons. Once the first road of the sidings had been filled, a bunker operative would uncouple, the guard would send the train forward, set the points for the next road and call the train back again. The empties would normally be accommodated in the sidings within two or three of these shunts.

Whilst the secondman secured Street Lane, the guard would uncouple the front brakevan and the loco would propel it into the loop with the other one. The loco would then run round the brakevans and draw them both back through Denby North to a point roughly 50 metres away from Kilburn gates, where the rear brakevan would be uncoupled. The loco and remaining brakevan would continue forward through Kilburn gates and the secondman would operate the ground frame and set them back onto the loaded train. Once coupled, the whole thing would be drawn over Kilburn

Crossing, leaving the guard to roll his brakevan onto the back of the train. This was a move that was preferable to get right first time, as you didn't want to stop short or bounce off the buffers, particularly with the waiting motorists as an audience.

May 1991 saw the introduction of a rapid loader, making the whole operation a lot easier by rendering Street Lane Crossing, the sidings, and all the intensive shunting obsolete. On arrival at Denby, the loco (now usually a Class 56) would be set on slow speed and the empty wagons simply drawn through the rapid loader, under instruction from the bunker operative. The secondman would still open Denby North gates, but only at the last minute, as the train made its snail-like progress towards Street Lane Crossing and the buffer stops just before it. I often thought the contradiction of having a rapid loader that you went slow speed through vaguely amusing, but none of the waiting motorists at Denby North ever did.

It gets dark at 16:00 at this time of year and I sometimes wonder how we ever made it off the branch in time, particularly when you consider that our signing on time was 12:22. Even on a good day, we probably wouldn't relieve the Toton crew until at least 13:00, so not counting any other delay or unforeseen difficulties en-route, that only gave us a maximum three-hour window to clear the branch. With the rapid loader in operation, our new signing on time became 11:47, but as Toton began squeezing in two morning trips, instead of one, our afternoon job obviously had to be held at Little Eaton Junction until they cleared the branch. Therefore, even with the more efficient rapid loading method, our already brief window of opportunity never really improved.

As I continue towards where the rapid loader used to be sited, a 42 MGR sign lurks in the undergrowth, signifying that the rear of the train was clear of Kilburn Crossing. It also signifies the end of the walk, at least as far as the Denby Branch is concerned anyway, as a spiked metal fence prevents further progress. I temporarily rejoin the road again to visit Denby North Crossing.

There is a small green space (the Drury-Lowe Millennium Green – named after one of the major landowning families, and former colliery in the area), between Denby North and Street Lane Crossings and all is relatively quiet as I stand there now. Back then however, there was the constant noise of industry; the creaking and screeching of coal hoppers, the reversing alarms of the giant tippers on the opencast site and the endless scraping of digger buckets and conveyor belts – even the lunch-time whistle at Denby Pottery played a part in this ghastly industrial orchestra. I suppose the peace and quiet would be much appreciated by the old boys after all that noise, effort and hustle and bustle of life. But speaking as one of those old boys, if I listen hard enough, I can still hear the sweet, hypnotic turbo-charged whistle of a pair of Class 20s shuttling in the background...but it's just another echo. An echo from a time when coal was still king, and perhaps, for a moment, I was too.

There is little evidence of the headshunt beyond Street Lane, but in the fields to the rear of the houses, it is possible to discern a line of trees that mark the former route and still find scattered railway ballast amongst them. Train crew didn't have 42 MGR signs to rely on before 1992, so wedged – now embedded – in one of these trees is a brick and a BR chair bolt. There is roughly a train length between here and Park Hall Sidings head points, so when the loco cab was level with this ad hoc marker, the driver could reasonably assume that the rear of the train was in clear. Perhaps, in years to come, people might wonder why this tree was singled out...now they will know!

Beyond Street Lane headshunt is an over bridge, which carried a private branch of the gangway over Bottle Brook into Denby Pottery. Former gangway gritstone sleeper blocks still lie scattered beneath. It seems strange to me that remnants of the earliest form of railway (of anywhere in the world!) just lie discarded in a brook.

For the train crew, it would be a return journey along the branch and a repeat of its many crossings, but for me, I continue along the road (the B6179 mirrors the route almost in its entirety) past Denby Pottery, until I reach Marehay, where I join the Greenway path and walk the remainder of the Ripley Branch to Hammersmith. The railway may be long gone on this stretch, but there are still a few pubs to visit.

The author is in contemplative mood as 56020 approaches Denby North Crossing, January 1992. *Jim Riley*.

6. BRAKEVAN RULES!

Whenever I tell people that 'modern' trainmen were still riding around in brakevans right up until industry privatisation in 1994, even on fully fitted freight trains, I am often met with disbelief.

Guards' brakevans were still being used on trains, but only on two specific types: ones carrying dangerous goods and ones that were unfitted (i.e., without functioning train brakes). However, a noteworthy addition to this was our very own Denby Disposal Point-Willington Power Station job – another of the previously mentioned fully fitted freight trains. Two brakevans were necessary on this train, simply because of the trainman operated crossings along the branch. (There were also plough brakevans on certain ballast trains, but the guard was not required to ride in these).

The three categories of dangerous goods where a brakevan would be required were nuclear flasks, hydrocyanic acid and toxic gas. The reason for having one on this kind of work was quite simple, if a problem occurred with the train (e.g., a fire or derailment), the driver would go forward to carry out detonator protection, whilst the guard, who was already at the rear, would go back. That way, no one would have to pass any potentially unstable or damaged wagons, which was rather important considering the nature of the materials being conveyed. Unfortunately, this strategy didn't consider wagon damage occurring within a tunnel. With the through draught in one direction only, either the driver or guard would not emerge alive, so before embarking on these jobs, the designated crew were often jokingly asked if they had bought a canary along for advanced warning.

The reason for having a brakevan on unfitted, or partially fitted trains was, that if a coupling broke and the train became divided, the driver would be able to apply the loco brakes and stop the front portion, whilst the guard would apply his brake and stop the rear portion. An important thing to remember, which could easily be overlooked in all the excitement, especially for trainmen who spent most of their time on fully fitted trains, was that the train was unbraked. So, before anyone set about uncoupling the loco or brakevan, it was wise to apply at least one handbrake somewhere. More than once, a trainman has been witnessed sprinting after runaway locos or rolling stock – rolling being the operative word.

As well as the Denby-Willington, train crew at Derby 4 Shed were also blessed (or cursed, depending on how you felt about brakevan work) with two toxic gas jobs (York and Bromsgrove respectively), plus occasional movements of unfitted London Underground stock (Litchurch Lane-Landor Street-Litchurch Lane), as well as the odd preserved or condemned loco or stock transits. Two good examples from the latter category were the movement of preserved diesels from Peak Rail (Matlock) to Leicester for the depot open day, and the removal of the scrap Class 45s from Egginton Junction to Toton in 1992.

Unfitted trains were restricted to 25mph and partially fitted to 35mph, which could be laborious on any journey over five miles – for the train crew and the relevant signalmen! On the 'Denby' the permissible speed was 45mph, and on our two dangerous goods jobs, 60mph. A rough analogy of the latter would perhaps be to imagine standing through the sunroof of a car that is last in a line of fourteen cars all chained together and doing the national speed limit. The Millennials would despair too; no toilet, electric, water, comfortable seats or restraints, just hard surfaces and unyielding edges. It was no wonder that this type of work was often referred to as '14 times round the stovepipe and back in time for tea'.

It sounds comical now but there was a stove in every brakevan, and a more unsafe environment for one I could not conceive. The stove (including stovepipe) would invariably be glowing red and, as riding in a brakevan was akin to being on a fairground cakewalk, every bump and lurch had the potential to send you careering into it. However, when you consider that you were essentially travelling in a garden shed at speeds of up to 60mph, often attached to wagons containing hundreds of tonnes of flammable, explosive, toxic or radioactive material, I suppose first degree burns from the stove were of little consequence in comparison. I dread to think of the risk assessment and endless paperwork that would be required if you had to ride in one nowadays. Not forgetting that you were also carrying ten detonators around with you too. The legislation for the 'simple' act of breathing seems extensive enough now, never mind rattling around in a brakevan with a red-hot stove and ten little explosives.

Mentioning health concerns, it was better to be a smoker on this type of work and thus already be carrying matches or a lighter around – as opposed to a non-smoker that ordinarily would not have this equipment about their person – as there would often be the odd paraffin lamp that required the application of a naked flame. More important though, was the possession and maintenance of a good fire in the stove, especially if you required hot sustenance or just simple warmth and light during a shift. (I also used to take a candle for illumination...oh, the deprivation!) Therefore, smoking just became an enjoyable, if unhealthy pastime to carrying the necessary ignition equipment around. It may also have helped relieve some of the stress and boredom of brakevan travel too. (I was a cigar man, just for the record.)

The ride was a little better on fully fitted trains, but the odd violent snatch could still catch you out, not to mention unexpected occurrences. Such was the case when the driver on the 'Denby' accidentally pressed the parking brake button instead of the brake overcharge button in the Class 58 that was heading the train and catapulted the unsuspecting guard from one end of the brakevan to the other.

Similarly, I was once on the York job, rattling happily behind twelve Chlorine tanks, when the train came to a juddering halt in the middle of Clay Cross Tunnel (1 mile, 24 yards long, in case readers were wondering). Obviously, there were no mobile phones back then, so I was unable to communicate with the driver to ascertain the problem, but as the air brake gauge currently read zero that seemed a likely place to start. However, rules dictated that I first place a track circuit operating clip on the adjacent line and start walking back with my detonators; my raison d'être. As I was contemplating this dark and perilous walk, I heard the air pressure building up again and just managed to jump onto the brakevan as it lurched clumsily away. I had suspected that the driver's foot had momentarily slipped off the DSD pedal and my suspicions were proven correct upon arrival at York.

Assorted brakevans at Toton, April 1995. Air piped only brakevans for the 'Denby' were easily identifiable by their yellow panels. *Richard King*.

The flame has gone out and the fire has died – although this could be a potential disaster in a single brakevan, it also serves as an adequate metaphor for their demise as a whole. The brakevans are no more – what a shame...depending on how you felt about them of course! For my part, I enjoyed their novelty and to experience their final years on British railways. *Author*.

ABOUT THE AUTHOR

Tim Helme was born in Derby and raised in Derbyshire. More truant than student, he joined the Junior Leaders aged sixteen, then later, the regular Forces. Turning his back on a promising military career, he joined British Rail in 1990 to follow his true calling of railwayman, but this aspiration was cut short owing to industry privatisation in 1994. He then followed the well-trodden paths of security, building and groundwork, interspersed with several years' truck driving. The Epilogue of *Derby Trainman* proved surprisingly prophetic, when he returned to the railway in 2006. He is currently serving as a signalman on the North Staffordshire Line and working on his next book entitled:

Train On Line

Tim Helme (aka The Derby Trainman) was eventually reconciled with the railway, although not in a way he ever envisaged. Instead of returning to drive trains, he ended up signalling them. Working on the North and South Staffordshire Lines gave him time to reflect on life, both on and off the railway. Just what DID go on in all those little wooden boxes? Join him as he takes you on a journey into the funny, frustrating and sometimes poignant world of the signal box. Release date: To be confirmed.

GLOSSARY

AWS	Automatic Warning System
BIS	Battery Isolation Switch
CE	Civil Engineers
DSD	Driver's Safety Device
EMCC	East Midlands Control Centre
HST	High Speed Train
MGR	Merry-Go-Round
MoD	Ministry of Defence
PSB	Power Signal Box
PWay	Permanent Way
RMC	Ready Mixed Concrete
RTC	Railway Technical Centre
S&T	Signal & Telegraph (latterly Telecom)
TCS	Train Crew Supervisor
TMO	Trainman Operated Crossing
TOPS	Total Operations Processing System
TPO	Travelling Post Office

Printed by Amazon Italia Logistica S.r.l.
Torrazza Piemonte (TO), Italy